The Boys of The Millennium

Rj Pettinelli

NEW HARBOR PRESS

RAPID CITY, SD

Pettinelli/New HarborPress
1601 Mt. Rushmore Rd, Ste 3288
Rapid City, SD 57701
www.newharborpress.com

Ordering Information:
Quantity sales. Special discounts are available on quantity purchases by corporations, associations, and others. For details, contact the "Special Sales Department" at the address above.

The Boys of The Millennium/Rj Pettinelli. -- 1st ed.
ISBN 978-1-63357-464-9

To my Mom. Who is up in heaven right now elbowing all the other inhabitants and saying, "That's my daughter. She wrote a book!"

The rise and fall of your God will tell me the story of your city. The rise and fall of your faith will show you the things I've been missing. Let the war begin.

—Kevin Martin

Contents

Prologue 3

    Reclamation 5

Part 1 7

    Dube 9

    Gaz 19

    Maj 27

    Vel 35

    Jae 41

    Grace and Harald 49

Part 2 51

    Dube 53

    Maj 61

    Gaz 69

    Vel 81

    Jae 89

    The Boys 97

Endnotes 105

Acknowledgements 107

Prologue

Reclamation

AS A VERY YOUNG child, I thought it strange that wisps of grass were called *"blades."* The first time I heard it I cried and wriggled out of my father's grasp when he tried to put me down on the neighbor's freshly-mown lawn. He smiled, that infinitely patient and wryly amused smile that only a loving father can manage, and lightly passed his hands over the soft tendrils. I hesitated, then gingerly did the same and finally catapulted onto the green expanse, fell over and giggled around.

It was much later when I again considered the word *blade* as I told my last family of the hard surfaces that once covered the Earth. I realized then that nature always won in the end. After the first Event, those blades cut through even the most stubborn blacktop, cement, or paving, turning them into hard mosaics with soft green grout. Bit by bit, dividing, cracking, pulverizing; until eventually all was returned to the dust from which it was made; until a thousand years later, everyone walked only on downy surfaces, fragrant and growing. No child needed fear scraped knees or elbows in the inevitable fall.

If only all falls were so lacking in consequence . . . .

Part 1

Dube

THE BROADSWORD FELT COMFORTABLE in Dube's hands, a close companion he would be lost without. The fiery-haired apparition was coming at him fast. Dube lifted the sword and swung, faintly aware of the sound of the blade slicing through the air, completely concentrated on the moment when the blade met its mark. As the apparition fell, he heard, "Dube! Breakfast!"

Just as if he had done this a thousand times before—which he had—Daniel Uzziah Benjamin Ezekiel groggily replied, "Just five more minutes!" But this time he had a reason. His recurring nightmare had changed. Was it because of the practice he had been putting in with Jae in swordsmanship? Was it his parents' assurances that his future would be successful no matter what he decided to pursue? Whatever it was, killing the beast in the dream was such a relief after what felt like millennia of being the one sliced and bleeding on the ground, watching his failed life play out before his eyes.

Almost true to his word, Dube lay in bed for another ten minutes looking around his room. The walls were covered in a paper illustrated with mechanical drawings of buildings, a nod to his father using this as a study before Dube took it over. Because it was an attic room, there were dormer windows interrupting the perfect slope of the ceiling, a ceiling that Dube frequently bumped into but tolerated because it put him farthest from the rest of the family and gave him the privacy he longed for. Still, the room was warm, filled with all of Dube's books, clothes, swords, and sports gear. Sure, most of it was on the floor but that's the way he preferred it.

His parents had chosen this BE dwelling—historically called a "Painted Lady"—in Nusan, over the multi-block apartments where most of his friends lived. The multi-blocks were so convenient—all of the maintenance and surrounding parkland was kept by the associations. Dube and his family had to clean, paint, plant, mow the walks, and fix whatever broke. Even now, Dube saw that the dormer window was covered in condensation, which meant he and his mother would be caulking sometime soon. His siblings had been happy to spend time with mom or dad puttering around the antique they lived in. Being the last one to leave—the youngest—had definite disadvantages for the only member of the family who was generously described as "the one with brilliant impracticable skills."

Dube unfolded his six-foot-two-inch lanky frame from the bed—his height, one of the reasons he frequently sparred with the ceiling. He checked his image in the mirror. He had his father's strong features but his mother's dark coloring. He often wished he were towheaded like his older siblings with his father's deep blue eyes. He was certain he would have been more popular in basic school if he looked like his Scan ancestors. Instead, he spent most of his school days studying and hanging out only with his best friend, Jae. At least Gaz was darker than Dube, not really the reason he had gravitated toward his Soasind friend, but a bonus, nonetheless.

Dube threw on jeans and a T-shirt and shuffled downstairs to the breakfast table. Like the rest of the house, the kitchen looked ancient, warm, and somewhat cluttered. The walls and cabinets were painted white but the accents of tile and appliances were red and cheerful. The old gas stove had been replaced with a nuclear version, but even that had been modeled to look like an old gas stove. There had been a wave of nostalgia in the past few decades that culminated in modern decor that looked ancient. His mother, Grace, had remodeled the house in retro style, replacing all the old appliances, fixtures, and surfaces with new ones that looked exactly the same but performed better. Dube thought it was a waste of time and funds, but never said so aloud because he was pleased when his mother was happy. He just tried not to show it.

Grace was humming around the kitchen while Harald sat at the red-and-white diner-style table reading the latest from Cole's council. Grace was a small woman with birdlike bones that belied her physical strength. Her hair was dark but only because of periodic salon visits. She had recently denounced the gray that was her natural color. Dube knew that soon she would tire of the maintenance and go back. Grace was not really vain but having one son still at Uni made her feel out of place amongst the younger mothers.

Harald was the reason for Dube's height. At six-foot-four he towered over Grace, but always said his life purpose was to reach high shelves for her. At five-foot-one-and-one-fourth-inch, Grace could barely reach her husband's or son's cheek to kiss. But she often said, "Lean over," to playfully smack the back of one of their heads for some sarcastic remark. Harald was also where Dube got his snark.

Harald adored Grace and she him.

Grace laid a red porcelain bowl of manna in front of Dube. She frequently prepared the honey-flavored cereal because it was nutritious and she said it reminded her of all the family had been and had been given. Dube liked it well enough, but could have skipped the usual lecture about his heritage and how it should help decide his Purpose.

"Now son," Harald droned on, "you are a privileged child and along with that privilege . . . ."

". . . *goes great responsibility,*" droned in Dube's head. Actually, the sentence could have ended with ". . . *you get egg roll,*" because Dube had stopped listening. He sighed to himself. He was coming up on his thirtieth birthday, and well aware that he had to decide what to pursue in life. He was nearly finished with Uni and, although some continued to become professors, he wasn't sure if that should be his fate, too. Dube and his friends from Uni all had developed a studied indifference about their Purpose. None of them had declared—which wasn't unusual for their age—but none had even narrowed their field of interest. It was probably the one thing that brought them together as a group. Dube was certain that fate had a plan for him and just as certain that it would be revealed at the right time. He had seen it in so many students in the older classes and even in his own family. Maybe that was what all of his friends were waiting for.

His friends consisted of a group that ironically called itself "The Boys." His friends! Dube jumped up from his half-finished manna as he remembered he was supposed to join Jae, Vel, and Maj at the transfer port down the block. Gaz would be vizing in from Soasind at any minute, and they wanted to meet him. Although Gaz lived in Nusan, he frequently visited his extended family and came back smelling and looking like the colorful, aromatic culture of his parents. Try as he might, he couldn't get home fast enough to change and shower because his friends were always at the port to embarrass him.

Dube interrupted his father's lecture with a quick, "Gotta go!" He grabbed his mother's freshly baked naan to eat on the way, shrugged into his bright green backpack, and darted out the door. Cries of "Wait, where are you going?" and "We aren't finished with this conversation!" vapor-trailed behind him. It wasn't lost on Dube that he was going to ride Gaz mercilessly about his ethnic customs and comestibles while digesting the very same.

As Dube left the porch of the house and stepped onto the grass walk, he slowed down. He wasn't actually late to meet Gaz, but he was eager to leave the house and stop the lectures and inevitable arguments they brought. He kicked off his sandals and let the dewy morning grass cool his feet. It was early enough that the trees were still glowing. He recalled history lessons about the introduction of bioluminescence into plant life. It was hard to imagine artificially lit streets and hard surfaces, even with some images available. The soft grass and glow of trees and plants were so soothing that Dube was sure it would be stressful to be out at night with harsh streetlights and concrete. Grace spent as much time as possible outdoors, especially at night; she said she was enthralled by the soft light, green carpeting, and cool breezes that always wafted in after sundown. Dube used to love spending time with Grace in the evenings, and a twinge of regret nagged at him that he hadn't done so in a long time. But while Grace was less lecture-prone than his father, she was still surreptitiously trying to push him into making a decision. Somehow, that was worse.

Thinking about his mother reminded Dube of his family's history and name. The Neuwirth house wasn't the only thing that was old-fashioned.

Before, the Event people had picked random single names and always used their surname or last name. After the Event, the Registry had formed quickly and everyone was asked, but not ordered, to use acronames—a short name formed by using the first letters of three- or four-part biblical given names. Surnames could be used, but were not necessary. In the ancient past, surnames were a way to identify lineage or even the trade of the owner or the region where they lived. Almost everyone born after the Event didn't lay stock in clans, ancestry, or birthrights. They were either called Earthers or Hume, named to delineate the boundaries of their existence. No one worked to pay for shelter and sustenance now. Cole gave these basic necessities and more to all Hume.

Grace and Harald Neuwirth had given all of their children acronames, while keeping the old names themselves. When Dube had pressed them for their reasons as a young child, his mother simply said *"dark mirrors."* The scripture reference he had learned in Bible class didn't clarify that at all. After a lot of frustration, Dube learned to let it be. As he got older, he realized that there was some speculation among the Neuwirth's friends as to why Dube's parents had opted to keep their surname, but Grace would never explain.

It was frustrating for young Earthers to use Old Earth names as they tried to make acronames out of them and usually failed. Consider Rachel Pirello, for example—Grace often talked about her long-since transitioned friend with the old-style name. With no middle name or names, her acroname would end up being Rp. How would you pronounce that: *Erp? Rip? Rup?*

There were those born BE that had been transformed at the time of the Event and didn't need food or a place to live. They were called by their Old Earther names but referred to by the genderless pronoun *seh*. As a group, they were ironically called *Ang*, based on the old beliefs that those who transitioned or were transformed became angels. Everyone knew this wasn't true: Angels were a totally different being and were not transitioned Hume. If Dube had propagated that falsehood, Dr. Jay would have sat him down for a very long lecture. Thinking of his advisor reminded Dube that he had decisions to make about his future. He quickly tried to fill his mind with anything else.

Jae was first at the vizport, as he usually was. Like Dube's parents, Jae's wanted him to "do something". So, the questions and urgings started during breakfast and continued throughout the day. In their way of thinking, Dube and his friends weren't yet finished with Uni, and there was no rush to find their calling. Jae had told Dube he was hoping his calling was hanging with the Boys.

Jae was complaining, as he usually was. There was no greeting when he saw Dube, no pleasantries, not even a morning grunt like Vel. The first thing out of Jae's mouth was a "What do they want from me?" whine.

On days like this, Dube didn't hesitate to act.

"Jonathan Abraham Enoch!" Dube squeaked in his best imitation of Jae's mother. "You have a gift from Abba! You can't waste your short two-hundred-forty-five years on this planet hanging with that group of no-lifes. You need to DO! You need to BE! You must

PURPOSE! We didn't raise you to waste LIFE. Start NOW!" And, as usual, Jae laughed at Dube's uncanny mimic ability.

'What's so funny? C'mon, share!" Vel urged, with Maj close on her heels. The two women joined in while all four continued trading complaints, waiting for the transfer, waiting for their group to be complete.

The Boys had formed more or less organically, but calling themselves *"Boys"* was very much on purpose. The irony of the name was that Vel, a female, had suggested it. She had been watching entertainment vids at the Old Earth Museum and heard the phrase. It had made her laugh at the time, and smile every time she heard it for a long while after. Despite the obvious physical differences, Earthers got the same ed, the same opportunities and equal treatment, whether male or female. And the Boys were so alike in their ideas and desires that they had naturally stayed together after they found each other. Part of Dube's reluctance to choose a Purpose could be traced back to his fear that the Boys would have to go their separate ways eventually. And he definitely wasn't ready for that.

Mostly Dube's reluctance was based on his fear of losing out. Suppose he decided to become a sword-warrior? The idea of guarding the temple was appealing, and Dube was very good at swordsmanship. It was mostly an honorary position as the warriors never engaged in battle. Who was there to fight? All Hume revered and obeyed their generous and kind leader, Cole. The minor infractions that happened when someone was jealous or greedy or selfish were dealt with immediately by the judges, and punishment was lenient, usually just extra workdays in your housing block. So, the sword-warrior position consisted of battle practice, camaraderie, and some standing guard at the temple doors. But all sword-warriors were pledged to celibacy, and what if Dube wasn't happy being a single person in the guard? Maybe he should be a Uni history instructor, going home every night to a family. Or, what about a field biologist or electronic specialist? Dube had many things he was decent at—in some, he excelled and had more interests that he had never explored.

His reverie was broken by Gaz appearing in the vizport kiosk. Dube's first thought when he saw Gaz was how unremarkable it was that he should travel thousands of miles in mere seconds. His second thought was how Grace and sometimes Harald were still astonished at this mundane fact. And then the look on Gaz's face stopped his thoughts cold.

"It's a catastrophe!" Gaz howled. "I'm engaged!"

CHAPTER 2

Gaz

GABRIEL ABSOLOM ZEPHANIAH LOOKED defeated, but only to Dube and only for a second. The rest of the Boys saw the expression of defiance that was Gaz's uniform. Dube was concerned that his friend may have finally been undone by his parents' overzealous meddling.

"Come with me to the Reg?" Although it was a question, it sounded like a command.

Dube stopped worrying and replied, "Of course."

The Registry was a set of buildings placed all over the world, with the Main one found here in Nusan. The rules were that business incorporations, partnerships, local elders, and the like could register anywhere in the world, but you had to come to the Main to register births, deaths, marriages, and occasional divorces. Since everyone on Earth needed to come to this one office at some time in their life, there was a vizport right outside the entrance.

Actually, the entire Main was a sort of vizport. The building itself looked huge, but the door opened to one large, well-lit room. Since all Reg employees were Ang, they knew why you were there, and the room was decorated accordingly. Ang could read Hume minds, but they weren't allowed to by Cole on any occasion, except when employed by the Reg. Wedding Reg rooms had lovely bell music and gauzy fabric draped around, usually in the colors you chose for your ceremony. Transition Reg rooms were of two types. Some were somber, in dark colors with soothing music. Those were for the Hume who were still a bit sad that their loved one had been transformed and would no longer be with them in their daily life. Others were wildly decorated with lively music—Newor-style funeral marches or Ang harp concertos—to celebrate the loved one's passage and release from human frailty. No matter how the room looked, there was only one sitting area, a few chairs, a sofa or two, and tables for the Ang and Hume to conduct business.

When Gaz opened the door, Dube gasped, then quickly hid his surprise. The room was smaller than he usually saw it, with only the table and chairs, and no decor. The Ang had a look that was hard to determine. Was it stern and judgmental or sympathetic? It wasn't any more clear when seh spoke.

"So, Gaz, you want to terminate your engagement?"

"Yes, sir. Is that possible?"

"All things are possible, but not all are beneficial"[2]

"So, you think I should stay in this arrangement?" The earlier deferential tone in Gaz's voice was wearing thin.

"Consider all the thought and prayer that went into it. Your parents and Sim's consulted Cole's best counselors. They talked to you many times to determine what your life Purpose might be, and who you would enjoy sharing life with. You probably didn't know that was their intent, but it was. Sim was also consulted to make sure the arrangement was pleasing to her. This was not entered into lightly, and should not be terminated lightly. At the very least, Sim should join you here for the ending instead of Dube."

"Dube and I are bests and he understands me!" Gaz practically growled. "I want to terminate, and you need to complete that right now. No one, not my parents, or Sim or her parents, gets to tell me what is right for me. I decide."

The outburst didn't surprise Dube at all. Gaz, despite his large, close-knit family, or possibly because of it, had always protected and served himself first.

Gaz and Dube had met in a biology class. The class had been a last-minute addition to Dube's schedule that ended up being one of the best indecisions he had ever made.

When he arrived on the first day of class, Dube scanned for someone who looked smart and hard-working. Dube wasn't necessarily lazy, but usually needed a push to get started and complete projects. He did want to do well in school and had learned to lean on others in subjects that were outside his comfort zone. He recognized some fellow slackers and waved weakly. Then he spotted someone who was diligently checking the online class info.

The boy, well, really a man, had dark curly hair hanging just below his browline. It gave the impression of a devil-may-care attitude, but that was contradicted by everything else about his demeanor. His deep brown eyes were sharply focused on the page. He was casually dressed in jeans and a cotton button-down shirt, but they were neat and wrinkle-free, unlike Dube's. He sat with a straight back with trainer-clad feet firmly planted on the floor. In other words, he looked like an excellent opportunity for passing the class.

Dube checked the class roster and believed he knew the name.

"Gaz, isn't it? Studying to be a doctor? I'm sure mommy and daddy would be pleased at that."

Gaz grunted in response, his eyes registering contempt for only a second before returning to his reading.

Dube took the hint and tried not to irritate Gaz any further. "Do you know anything about this prof? I needed a science credit, but this was the only thing available that fit into my schedule."

Gaz looked up, confused for a moment, but then seemed to relax. "Yeah, this prof is great. You're lucky to get Bio from her. It's one of my favorite subjects, but she makes it even more interesting. I sat in on all the Bio 1 classes last semester. I didn't want some lit prof ruining it for me, and Prof Set is all science."

"So, do you have a lab partner yet? I promise I'm not a Liberal Arty kind of guy." Dube noticed the slight smile and figured his charm was working at least a little.

"Sure, why not. I'm taking this class out of the trad order, so I don't know anyone here. Just don't start writing poetry about the dissection dummy, and we'll be fine."

"Oh, dummy fair of bod and face. With organs strewn all over the place." This drew an actual smile from Gaz. Dube figured he was home free.

Prof Set started with the introduction to the class. Dube listened enough to get the basics, but knew the information would be online, just as he had seen Gaz checking it before class. Surprisingly, the prof had also printed up papers. She handed them to a woman who was sitting in the front row.

Dube studied her as she handed out the pages. She was tall and powerfully built. He scanned his memory and thought he recognized her from a sports team, but he didn't remember which one. Her blond hair was cut short, befitting someone who needed to be unencumbered. She had those watery blue eyes that spoke of Eastern European heritage from Old Earth. As she approached them, she smiled at Gaz.

"Hi, Gaz. I'm glad we have this class together. Do you have a lab partner yet?"

"Oh, Vel, I apologize. I know we said we'd pair up in any science class but . . . uh . . . I don't know your name . . . ."

"Dube."

"Yeah, Dube asked first."

Just then, Prof Set broke in. "We have enough drops that the class is uneven. Would anyone volunteer to work a team of three?"

Gaz stood. "Professor, we'll work together. Vel, Dube, and Gaz."

And that was the beginning.

"Dube, I asked what you thought." The Ang wasn't irritated when seh had to ask a second time. But then, mind-reading was helpful in this situation. Seh got to see that Dube loved Gaz and was looking out for him. Even though at their first meeting Dube was definitely looking out for himself.

"Gaz has always been driven and knows what he wants. Tradition and parents notwithstanding, I think his instincts here are good. Let him break the engagement. Sim will most likely be miserable if Gaz is forced to go through with the marriage, and none of us wants a divorce. I'm guessing, especially Cole."

"All right," the Ang intoned sadly. For a brief moment, Dube got the strange feeling that this was not over—that the Ang saw a future wrinkle. Dube let the feeling pass. He was prone to these moments but—and despite his mother's encouragement and delight—he usually ignored them.

Gaz was a free man again.

Dube and Gaz made their way back to the other three. There was a cacophony as everyone asked what happened, how Gaz was, who he had been engaged to, and how the Ang took the reversal. Vel and Jae were voicing their opinions that Gaz had done the wrong thing.

"Seriously, dude, you shouldn't have acted so fast. You know sleeping on things is always a good idea," Jae warned. "Your parents and Cole only want the best for you. And you need to honor them—Cole, especially. What does He say about . . . ?

Vel interrupted. "My parents always say, `Haste makes waste.' Mom actually knitted that into my scarf here! Of course, they are usually talking to me, but I think it applies here. You know we love you, brother, but you just had a shock. Although your instincts are usually good, maybe you could have talked to us first about why you wanted to break the engagement?"

"Mostly," Gaz answered wearily, "because I'm old enough to make my own choices. I want to marry when and who *I* want."

Vel jumped in with a snarky remark, as usual, "Are you sure you're old enough?" To which Jae replied, "It is better to live in a corner of the roof than in a house shared with a contentious woman.³" Which, of course, resulted in a head slap from Vel, who was taller and more agile, even as Jae tried to bob and weave.

Then, Maj finally spoke. "Yes, Gaz, we get it. But what about your parents? Don't you think they will be hurt?"

Gaz looked stricken. "Yes, they will be. It's really my only regret. But maybe this will finally get them to stop making choices for me. I've been telling them for years to let me decide. Now, they have no choice." Gaz's visage hardened as he went on. "My life, my future, my decision! They need to stop interfering. I'm old enough. I decide! Enough talk. Let's go!"

Maj

MIRIAM ANNA JEDIDAH COCKED her head and looked at Gaz as if she knew what he was thinking. And she probably did. She was the worrier of the group, but along with that propensity to dwell on things in her head, she seemed to be able to read people quite well. And her kind and optimistic nature made her a comfort rather than a confrontation when she knew exactly what you were thinking.

The Boys started walking toward NuPark for a game of Frisbee. Dube had found an ancient disc in the basement of his house and asked his parents what it was.

Grace looked at Dube without seeing him, a faraway, dewy look in her eyes. Harald nudged her affectionately as he said, "It's called a Frisbee, son. You throw it back and forth like a ball, but it has a different arc and sails through the air if you do it correctly. It does take some practice, but we can try it together. Your mom and I loved to go to the park—it was called Golden Gate then—and toss it around."

Grace returned to the present and added, "Dogs love to play catch with them. We once had a golden retriever named Gate. It was a sad attempt at humor."

Since that day, the Boys had taken up Frisbee with a passion. They played every chance they could. Everyone had gotten pretty good at throwing it, but Maj was the real star. Which was curious since Vel was the athlete of the group. Maj had taken up the game with abandon, and it seemed like one of the few times she was relaxed, free, and outside her head.

In a way, Maj had been the last of the Boys to be "found." It wasn't like they had actually looked for her, or anyone else. The Boys had formed effortlessly as each person came to know the group and joined in.

Maj and Dube lived on the same block. They had known each other and been friends all their lives, but only hung out at various times for various lengths of time. Five or so years ago was one of the times when Dube had lost contact with Maj. She had been away at school. Both the school and the area of study—BE history—were her parents' idea. And pleasing them had been enough for a while. Until it wasn't.

Dube remembered finding Maj on the stoop of her house crying. Her copper-brown curly hair was lighter than his and was accented by green eyes. Maj's skin was the color of milky coffee. Since the Event, most people looked like Maj; that is, they had mixed race skin, hair, and eye colors. The prejudice and "them vs us" feelings had mostly disappeared over the many years of Cole's kind rule. The way of Cole was to love all people equally, no matter what their genes expressed.

Maj was slim and short, a contrast to the tall, powerfully built Vel. But both women had beauty that shone from within, and often told people they were twins just to mess with their heads.

Dube handed Maj a cloth handkerchief. She looked at it as if it were a foreign object, which it essentially was for her and most other people. "It's to wipe your eyes or blow your nose. Then do you want to tell me what's wrong?"

Maj blew her nose loudly, then looked at the handkerchief with appreciation and a bit of wonder. "Oh, Dube. I must look a mess! I just failed out of university."

"But you majored in history—I thought you loved it! You always did so well in basic."

"Mostly because I have a great short-term memory and aced tests. Since I hesitated to pick a major, my folks pushed me into history. But it was so hard to hear about the suffering, both of people and the Earth, before Cole ruled. BE, there was so much greed and selfishness. Humans treated Earth like they treated each other. What couldn't be used was subjugated for the benefit of those at the top. Earth before the Event was tired and oppressed."

Dube understood what Maj was talking about. He knew that the Earth he lived in was very different from BE, and it had taken many years to recover not only from the Event and what led up to it, but also the centuries of abuse she suffered under those who were supposed to care for her. Immediately following the Event, Earth was scorched and shaken in many places by the war. Abba and Cole took care of those places, assisted by the Ang. Earthers weren't allowed in these most devastated areas during restoration, and some myths and legends had arisen over the speed and ease with which these areas were healed.

Maj started talking again and interrupted Dube's thoughts. "With every class, I got more and more depressed until I just couldn't get up in the morning. And, of course, not going to class kind of ruins your chances of doing well on exams." Maj smiled ruefully. "It finally got so bad that Mom and Dad had to pull me out. Did you know that Earthers BE had to *pay* for schooling?! I was shocked when that came up in class. But I was so relieved that Mom and Dad didn't lose anything by my screwup."

Dube had a sudden thought to help his friend. "You know, I'm meeting Jae and some others today in the park. We're playing with this new thing I found in our basement called a `Frisbee.' Mom showed me how to throw it, but I'm not very good yet. Do you want to come? It could be a laugh."

Maj's face changed suddenly, and Dube knew she was touched by the offer and considering the distraction it would bring. Maj got up off the stoop, jostled Dube, and they started walking toward the park.

Maj asked playfully, "Want your snot cloth back?" To which Dube replied, "Eww!"

Dube shook himself back to the present and the Boys continued on toward the park and their game of Frisbee. Walking along the street with multiple conversations going they didn't notice for almost half a block that Maj wasn't with them. Dube had one of his odd feelings and stopped midsentence in his ramblings to Jae.

"Where's Maj?" Dube turned and saw that she was speaking to a couple sitting in front of their apartment block. The couple was quite old, Dube suspected one or both were near the end of their life, and the man had only one foot. It was unusual that his missing limb hadn't been restored, but it was a choice some took. Dube had often wondered why but hadn't ever dared ask someone about their choice.

"A case for forced transition if I've ever seen one." Vel didn't catch herself, but she quickly covered her mouth with her hand and thankfully didn't continue speaking. The other three frowned slightly at Vel but didn't say anything further. Some Hume did believe that in a world so beautiful and peaceful, there was no room for suffering or pain. But that was not Abba's choice. Vel was entitled to her opinion, even if it seemed less than loving. And the Boys had long ago learned that Vel's speech could be unfiltered. They tried to help her to be kinder. It didn't always work.

Dube made his way back to Maj just in time to see her hand the couple something from her backpack, although he couldn't see what. Maybe a kudo? Then she bent down to hug them and turned around so quickly that she almost bumped into him. He noticed the tears in her eyes but didn't comment. Maj had a very soft heart. He decided to lighten the mood to help Maj recover.

"This Frisbee won't play itself," he said with a shake of his head as if in judgment. Maj knew him well enough not to bite. She punched him on the shoulder so hard it hurt. She could be fierce when necessary.

As they walked back to join the group, Dube was reminded of their brief attempt at dating. It had seemed like a good idea at the time. They had grown up together and were comfortable with each other. They could skip that awful, awkward phase in a new relationship. They could be silent in each other's company without scrambling to find something to say.

They went out to a restaurant that was fancier than the Boys usually frequented. They both felt a bit self-conscious, but soon found their way.

"I must say, old chap, this is jolly good grub." Maj's imitation of an Old Earth Englishman was spot-on if not lexically correct.

"Pip pip and cheerio," Dube countered.

Maj collapsed in laughter. "That was the worst accent I have ever heard!" Dube feigned injured pride for a moment, but couldn't help laughing himself. And they settled into companionable silence again.

After dinner, Dube walked Maj to her door. There was a tricky moment when they decided how to end the date, but then both Dube and Maj leaned in for a kiss. It was a short peck, and they pulled back quickly and both made a face.

"It was like kissing my brother!" Maj whispered, mildly embarrassed. She needn't have been. Dube felt exactly the same. He drew her into a hug. "Let's not ever do that again!"

Maj stretched up and kissed him on the cheek, then got out her keys and opened the door. "See you, my friend."

Dube's musings about Maj in the past were interrupted by Maj herself in the present. "Maybe I'll play one-handed today to give the rest of you a chance."

She was, of course, rewarded with a chorus of "*Pfft*" and rolled eyes. Dube simply smiled. He loved the change in Maj since she had started hanging out with the rest of them. The friendship, dare he say love, that the Boys felt and displayed for each other helped all of them heal. Maj was braver and more confident in her talents and gifts lately. She was able to tell her parents finally what she was interested in and was planning on going back to Uni soon. This time her major would be counseling. "Even in a perfect world," she would say, "we imperfect humans need someone to listen to us now and then."

The Boys walked on toward the park as the soft grass underfoot muffled their steps. The sun was fully up, and the warmth it created was comforting. Jackets were sloughed off and stuffed into Dube's backpack next to the Frisbee. The breeze tousled the leaves in the trees, and the resulting soft shushing noise seemed to end conversations. But, in reality, everyone was simply enjoying the day.

Then it hit Dube like a thunderbolt. This was why he didn't want to decide on his Purpose. It was probably why none of the Boys had actually declared yet. They were a team, a family of misfits, closer than siblings because they had chosen each other. Who else would listen without judgment as Gaz rejected Sim and marriage? Who else would even try to comfort Maj when she had failed so spectacularly? Who else would put up with Vel and her gumball pronouncements, or Jae's endless scripture quotes? Comfort, acceptance, support: even in Cole's peaceful world, these were cravings of Earthers all over the planet. Why would the Boys give that up simply because society said they must?

"Race you to the meadow!" Dube heard but wasn't sure who said it. What did that matter? They all instantly caught the fever and started running, laughing, and gently shoving each other out of the way.

It was Jae who expressed the essence of Dube's feeling with another of his biblical quotes: "There is a friend who stays closer than a brother."[4]

But Vel voiced everyone else's thoughts as she said, "Last one to the park is a rotten egg!"

Vel

IT WAS THE PERFECT pronouncement from Vashti Elizabeth Leah.

Grace had nailed Vel's nature with a quote from an old movie called *The Four Seasons*: "You think whenever your brain has a thought, it has to just drop down onto your tongue like a gumball." Vel never edited her thoughts well—or at all. It could be refreshing, irritating, hilarious, or downright mortifying. But it was the essence of Vel.

Tall and muscular, blonde with riveting blue eyes, Vel was beautiful in the classic sense. She didn't have a horde of would-be boyfriends, though, because she was so direct and intense. When she first excelled at sports in basic school, women and men used to flock around her. But slowly the crowds dwindled as she confronted some who had hidden plans for her, and others realized they couldn't conceal anything or have a quiet word with her that wouldn't be broadcast to the entire venue. Gaz, someone who went his own way in defiance of what others thought, embraced Vel almost to spite the exiting crowd.

The daughter of two famous athletes, Vel was the naturally gifted one. Her parents loved all of their children, even the clumsy Doa, but they had a special place in their hearts for Vel. Not only physically skillful, she was sharp mentally as well. It was one of Vel's parents' sticking points that she hung out with the Boys. They believed she was wasting her time and talent.

And why did she? For the same reason, with a different back story, as all of the others. They accepted her, didn't ask too much, and she could relax and stop being amazing for the hours she was with them.

The Bio class where Dube first found Vel turned out to be even better than his attempt to manage. Gaz and Vel were brilliant together. Dube could sit back and watch the two of them compete to come up with answers first, control the lab experiments, and write the class summaries. But he also sensed something in Vel that was amiss.

Dube often surreptitiously arranged time alone with a friend or acquaintance to talk to them. He was preternaturally curious about the feelings he had that something was not quite right in their world. Early in life, Dube felt this might make him a counselor, but quickly learned that the empathy he may have inherited from Grace made for sleepless nights any time he probed into someone's problems.

With Vel, however, there was no sneaking or arranging needed. She was waiting for him one day after class and just blurted it out.

"You seem to be so relaxed in class. I'm always worried my folks will be disappointed in me if I'm not the best at whatever I do. Even studies. Which is weird because they both did mediocre in school but always excelled in sports. Why do our parents push us to be better than them?"

Dube gestured to a bench in the corridor and then sat beside Vel.

"You know, you should join Jae and I sometime and just hang out. He's been my best friend since forever. Both of us have the same problem you are describing right now. Our parents are always pushing, pushing, pushing, and we feel like we just want to have time to decide, time to have fun and be together, before we choose a life path that may tear us apart. I'm meeting him today at the shops—would you like to come?"

"Really?" Vel said with obvious suspicion. "You're asking me to come with you and your best bud?"

Dube laughed inwardly, but arranged his smile and voice to be as welcoming as possible. "Absolutely! Jae will love you, and I'm already sold. Vel, I think this is the beginning of a beautiful friendship." Vel cocked her head and looked at Dube quizzically. Which made him realize that not everyone watched old, pre-E movies with their parents and popcorn most endweeks growing up.

"Never mind. Let's go"

Jae was waiting for Dube outside their favorite graphic novel shop. They had not agreed to meet today specifically, but since they knew each other's schedules and met most days, it was assumed. If something came up, they could always communicate regrets.

"Hey, Dube. And who is this lovely person?"

"Jae, meet Vel. She is graciously, and sometimes not so graciously, allowing me to cheat off her and Gaz in Bio, so I don't fail."

Vel laughed out loud at the very thing she might have said and opened her mouth to speak, but only got out a *"Very . . ."* before another voice interrupted.

"Did I hear my name taken in vain?"

"Gaz! What are you doing here?"

"Well, I came out of class wanting to talk over our next steps for an extra credit project and found my lab partners sneaking away without me. Imagine my hurt and the shock of seeing you two actually speaking to each other. Oh, the pain, the humiliation!"

"And the drama prize goes to Gaz—did I get that right?—for his performance in *Bio Class*, the movie." Jae made them all crack up. He was usually good for a laugh when he broke out of his super-serious persona. Jae, of all of them, really meant to do good, choose a life purpose well, and stay on track. Dube was a very bad influence on him, but one that probably added years to his life by distracting him from worry.

The group made their way to the cafe on the second floor of the shops and ordered coffee and terrible pastries. Dube knew his mother would have gladly hosted them with baked goods acknowledged to be the best in Nusan by anyone who was lucky enough to grab one before Dube. But he didn't want the questioning, the subtle directing, and the consternation it caused Jae.

"Wow—this is really disgusting!" Vel again.

"Yes, but it comes without lecture, expectation, and disparaging looks."

Vel didn't hesitate a moment. "Yum! So tasty!" Which, of course, caused the entire table to burst out laughing. And get sideways looks and outright stares. Which none of them minded in the least.

The group tried to lower their profile and their volume, so they could talk without being watched.

Dube was first by asking, "Does anyone mind if I text Maj and ask her to join us? I think she would be really pleased that we asked."

The chorus of agreement in various words and phrases made Dube really happy that this group was coming together. They all seemed to be accepting and easy with each other. He hoped this would be a pattern for a long time.

Vel spoke up next. "So, is this a regular thing, meeting up at horrible eateries and wasting your lives together?" The chorus of laughs and snorts was only mildly less loud than the last outburst, but thankfully drowned out by the squeal of milk steaming.

"I can answer that," piped in Maj, so close and silent on her approach that Jae started. "A definite yes."

"Hey, Maj," from Jae once he recovered. "That was really quick. Have you been shadowing Dube to see what nefarious plans he's up to?"

Everyone except Dube stared at Jae in disbelief and confusion. Dube tried to help out by explaining, "We watched an old detective movie with my parents last night, and Jae is still living in San Francisco in 1945."

Unfortunately, this was met with more confusion until Vel explained, "Humans on Old Earth used to pay someone to find another person or something that was stolen or to catch the 'bad guys,' whatever that meant. They were people called *detectives*. I've read some of the old books, and they're cool."

"So, how do you know about these books, Vel?"

"Well, Jae, I am socially awkward and introverted, so I read. A lot."

Jae thought for a minute and replied, "OK, then. You'll fit in perfectly."

CHAPTER 5

Jae

IT WAS SO JONATHAN Abraham Enoch to be kind. He often didn't know what to do himself, but was never deliberately mean. Jae was easy to overlook physically. Medium height, not tall like Dube, with medium brown hair, brown eyes, and brown skin. But if you took the time to know him you were never disappointed.

Jae was the son of parents who were as nondescript as he. Again, until you got to know them. As a Bible prof, his father, Dr. Pac, was a fiery presenter of Abba and Cole's Word. And he instilled a love of scripture into his son. But that also confused Jae. He saw so many examples of Cole directly telling His people what to do that Jae was expecting the same clear, miracle-based vision for his life. He often consulted with the Ang at the Registry, but the answer was usually the same. "You will know, Jae, when Abba and Cole want you to know." To another person, this would have been frustrating, but Jae had the patience of, well, a saint.

There was no hesitation when it came to his friendship with Dube. Jae was full in, fully invested, full of love for his friend. It was such a comfort to Dube—always relied upon, but never taken for granted. Dube made sure he, at least, took as good care of Jae as he felt he was given.

They had met in very early basic school. Dube was always tall for his age, and his dark features—and to be honest, his parents' reputation—made him feared just a little, even by the school bullies. One of them was picking on Jae the day he and Dube met.

Dube was on the other side of the playground but noticed someone being tormented, as he usually did. Grace and Harald had taught him to stand up for the weak, and his especially sensitive, almost mind-reading ability meant he did this on a regular basis. Dube had no idea that this time would be different.

Tru had knocked Jae's Bible to the ground with the particularly erudite taunt of *"Nyah nyah nyah!"* Dube looked over and noticed the chunky brown-haired Tru towering over a slight, bespectacled boy. He and Tru had history as Dube had interrupted his meanness many times. The bloody nose and black eye that Tru had suffered at Dube's fist had made the demerit in his school records totally worth it.

"Hey, Tru, what's up?" It wasn't a particularly frightening or forceful sentence, but Tru turned around with such a shocked look on his face that Dube was certain it was effective.

Tru tried hard to regain his composure. "What's it to you, Cole-pet?" The term was meant as a pejorative but was taken by many Earthers as a compliment.

"Just go, Tru. Before Cole sees." Dube, of course knew that Cole already saw. He didn't yet know the word *"omniscient"* but did know that Cole didn't miss a thing. And from his parents he was beginning to understand that Cole and Abba used Hume as their eyes, ears, and emissaries. Dube was particularly pleased when he was able to fulfill that role.

Tru slunk off muttering, "I'll deal with you later." Dube knew he wasn't in real danger. Bullies picked on those they could dominate. But just to mess with Jae one last time, Tru said, "And you, too!" Dube just rolled his eyes.

"Hi, I'm Jae. Thanks." Dube picked up and dusted off the Bible. It was well worn, a bit of an anomaly for an eleven-year-old. So, he commented on it as he handed it back.

"Yeah, my dad is a Bible prof and not very tall, so I had no chance to escape notice by Tru and his kind."

"I'm always a bit surprised by mean kids. I guess they have some reason to be like that, and Cole doesn't always stop it. Free will and all that . . . ."

"'Choose you this day whom you will serve.' That's from Joshua 24 . . ." Jae trailed off, embarrassed that he was once again nerding out over scripture. Dube, true to his nature, continued the quote to make Jae feel better: "But as for me and my house," until together they said, "We will serve the Lord." And laughed. For basic schoolers, both Jae and Dube were serious, introspective, and somewhat loners, so they got on well.

Dube would come to learn that Jae often quoted scripture, but never in a preachy way.

A few years after the Tru incident, Jae and Dube were out exploring, pretending they were part of Cole's army—although with peace reigning throughout the world, Cole didn't currently have an army—and hacking through brush in an undeveloped hilly area outside the city. As they came to the foot of a small rise and cleared away the foliage, they were surprised to see a cave. Even though they were in their early teens, Jae and Dube loved this kind of adventure out in the beautiful world Cole had created. They knew they would be safe and so decided to explore the cave further.

Turning on the electric torches they had brought, Dube led Jae into the darkness. Being a warm summer day, the coolness of the cave was refreshing. There was a fork in the cave, and Jae and Dube decided to each take a path. Dube made his way further into the cave, keeping his hand against the rough wall as he walked. He walked for a while, and for some reason, he started singing softly. *"Holy, holy, holy is the Lord God Almighty."* And to his great surprise, Dube heard Jae's clear tenor voice sing, *"Who was and is and is to come."*

And that's when it happened. The cave was suddenly filled with light and an angel—a *real* angel—appeared just in front of the dead-end of the cave. Of course, the angel's first words were, *"Don't stress! I'm here with good news"*—the modern equivalent of "Fear not! I bring you good tidings . . ." But even with the reassurance, Dube was awe-struck and immediately fell to his knees. Then the angel said the most confusing thing Dube had ever heard. "Don't forget this place. It will be important." And disappeared.

Jae came running up and shouted, "Dude!" Even as shocked as he was, Dube still managed the standard reply, "No, it's Dube." Dube and Jae laughed, as much from the relief as at the horrible stale joke.

"You saw that?" Dube queried Jae. And he answered, "Not saw as much as felt. I heard the words, and the light filtered into my side as well. What does it mean?" And Dube said the words he would repeat dozens of times, every time they came back to this cave and waited to see if anything would happen. "Man, I have no idea!"

When Jae started dating, Dube asked to come along so they could double. Dube, being the one who had a hard time making decisions, couldn't choose who to ask on a real date. And double dating made the terrifying experience enjoyable as the friends could jump in when one or the other did something awkward. Which happened a lot.

Like the time Dube forgot he had asked Maj to come for dinner and a movie at his house and then asked Eta. When Eta showed up early and rang the bell, Dube panicked.

"Oh man, I actually asked two girls to come with me tonight! Maj will be here any minute. Eta is a great practical joker, which means she will *never* let me live this down! What can I do?"

Jae thought for a second and then shoved Dube into the living room and told him to stay there. He then dashed into the downstairs bathroom and searched through the medicine cabinet, grabbed a bottle of pills, covered the label with his hand, and continued toward the front door. He drew on his theatrical abilities, put a pained look on his face, and answered the door as Eta knocked a second time.

"Oh, hi, Eta. I'm so sorry, but I have a migraine. I'm just about to take these pills and lie down. Dube is closing the curtains to make a dark room for me. He sends apologies and asks if he can call you another time?"

Eta looked at Jae suspiciously but decided he did look sick. "Sure, Jae, no problem. Tell Dube he's a good friend to take care of you. We'll try this again some time. Bye."

As she turned to walk back down the path she almost ran into Maj. The girls started to greet each other, saying hello and exchanging a friendly hug. Jae quickly called to Maj to keep her from saying too much to Eta, putting his arm around her, and guiding her into the house. To anyone watching, including Eta, it looked like Maj was Jae's date.

It didn't take Maj long to be suspicious herself. "What are you doing, Jae, and why do you have that bottle of Vitamin C?" Jae explained quickly, ending with the phrase ". . . and anyone can see that these are NoMoPain! For my raging headache. Which is actually coming on now that we are out of that potentially embarrassing situation."

Dube, watching the master at work the entire time, came out and wrapped his friend in a long hug, while saying hello to Maj over Jae's shoulder and asking, "Could anyone have a better friend?" Maj answered, "Not possible," while still not at all certain what had just happened. The doorbell rang again, and Maj went to answer it. She and Dube were in each other's houses so often that they would search each other's kitchens for snacks, riffle through closets for jackets when the weather turned, and yes, answer the door when someone was there.

The girl on the porch was so beautiful that Maj did a double take. Long, auburn hair, and bright hazel eyes, and just barely shorter than Jae, which still seemed to be the dating criteria even after a thousand years of equality. "Hi. I'm Esther. Am I at the right house? I'm looking for Jae."

Jae disentangled from Dube and said, "Hi! You are definitely in the right place. We're just a bit off kilter as my friend here caused a rift in the space-time continuum."

"Well," Esther replied, "We'll just have to fix that. Got a ship that can slingshot around the sun?"

And with that, Dube was certain that Jae would marry this girl.

As the Boys made their way to NuPark, Dube wondered again why Jae wasn't married and in training or already practicing a

Purpose. He often asked his friend but always got evasive answers. Esther—she of the old-fashioned name—had seemed to disappear one day and never returned. Nag, cajole, maneuver, grovel, or just ask straight out, Jae never told Dube what had happened. Although it was the rock in the shoe of their relationship, Dube had learned long ago to let it be.

When he and Jae were hanging out with his parents, the subject got even weirder. Grace and Harald lavished Jae with gifts and love, bugged him about selecting a Purpose, but never once asked why he hadn't married Esther. Dube's parents loved that girl like she was their own, and having an old name seemed to Dube to be one strange reason why. But Grace and Harald couldn't be bribed or guilted to say what they thought. They were like a stone wall.

CHAPTER 6

Grace and Harald

AND A STONE WALL is exactly where the Neuwirths found themselves this day as the Boys began their game of Frisbee. With blindfolds. Facing a camera and a firing squad. Holding hands. Praying to Abba that He would take care of Dube when they were gone.

And then they were. Gone, that is. Just vanished. You could have knocked Seo's soldiers over with a feather.

You see, Seo had been released from his prison only a few days ago. But it had taken no time at all for him to gather people who believed that he, not Cole in the name of Abba, was the rightful ruler. In the few days he had been free, he had spread lies and denigrations about the current ruler with the most foul language possible. Even some of Seo's followers were shocked, but it didn't stop them from doing what he wanted. A lot of that consisted of gathering those ultra-loyal to Cole and executing them. Most of the executions took place secretly. People just disappeared. It hadn't even been long enough for the disappearances to make a ripple in the news.

That changed with Grace and Harald. Seo wanted a tidal wave of shock when they died to help him gather followers. He blamed the Neuwirths in part for his incarceration. He knew that Neuwiths had helped hunt him and his followers after TE. The Neuwirth clan was famous right after the Event. Celebrated. But it had been a thousand years, and their fame had faded. Which suited Grace and Harald just fine. They liked living their simple life, training their family in the way they had done for years. But Seo had not forgotten. If anything, his hatred and enmity were sharper than ever. He would start with the Neuwirth clan and work his way up to Cole himself.

So, Grace and Harald put a giant kink in his plans by disappearing. Seo saw Abba's marks all over this incident, and it made him determined to go ahead in any way he could.

And so he did. He took the vid that they had of Grace and Harald and edited out their disappearance. Then he faked a new ending with actors where they were shot by a firing squad. Just to make sure it looked real, he actually executed the actors. What were two deaths compared to the glory of his return to power? Seo was so enamored with his triumph that he didn't notice one of his "soldiers" squirreling away the original footage on a storage device and silently making his way out of the compound.

And so it was that just a few short, terrible minutes later, Dube and his friends heard a news alert tone, and a vid screen appeared above the park.

Part 2

Dube

THE BROADSWORD FELT COMFORTABLE in Dube's hands, a close companion he would be lost without. The fiery-haired apparition was coming at him fast. Dube lifted the sword and swung, faintly aware of the sound of the blade slicing through the air when he felt a stinging sensation followed by intense agony that drove him to his knees. Collapsing to the ground, he saw a vision of Grace in her kitchen yelling up the stairs, "Dube, breakfast!" Only a second later, he woke up and realized that both Grace and the kitchen were no more.

Oh, hello. I'm going to take over now and tell you the rest of the story. By the way, I've noticed that many tellers address you as *Dear Reader.* But I don't even know you, so how can you be dear to me? You are reading our story, so I suppose you are interested in us in some way. Still, the phrase feels foreign on my tongue. And that's a very strange thing for me to say.

Anyway . . . .

Dube sat up and looked around the cave. The very cave he and Jae had found so many years ago. He hadn't been back in at least ten years and had to clear out the underbrush to get in last night. But he immediately felt the Ruler's presence and peace despite the awful memory of what had happened to his parents. And he was hopeful that the angel's words would finally make sense and that Jae would remember them and the cave as well.

Dube thought he would venture out and see what he could find for breakfast. Distraction would be good. He was also hoping against hope that Jae would find the rest of the Boys and bring them to this place.

After the awful vid had played out above them, Seo appeared on the vid screen and called out to Dube, "I hear you are an excellent swordsman, Dube. I can use you to help defeat Cole and restore my rule over the Earth. Stay there in the park, and I'll send someone to get you. But be warned! If you choose not to follow me, you will join your parents in death. I had my revenge on them for my unjust imprisonment. However, I am willing to give you a chance to atone for your parents' mistakes. If you are not for me, you are against me. Don't make that mistake as it will cost you and all of the Boys!"

The entire group was stunned. How did Seo know about them?

The others encouraged Dube to run and hide, saying they would scatter to try to distract Seo and his followers from finding him. They didn't know that Cole was with them at that very moment and hid each of them from sight. Even if Seo had been right next to Dube, he would never have seen him.

Cole was much more powerful than Seo, but the evil one wouldn't accept that. He was certain he could defeat Cole, and that his was the "right" way, the way that would make the Earth a great place to live. With everyone free from Cole's rules and rule, everyone free to take what they needed and more, and to avenge themselves against those who had wronged them, the Earth would be a glorious place to live.

At least for Seo and his followers. "Vengeance is mine says the Lord."[5] Well, thought Seo, that would no longer be true!

Dube, as quietly and carefully as possible, made his way to the mouth of the cave. No one was in there with him, and looking out, he didn't see anyone either. Still, he proceeded cautiously as Seo's threats were on his mind. As soon as he exited the cave, Dube was surprised to see a man in tattered clothing sitting outside with a bottle of nearly empty wine in his fist. He was grey-haired but with a sturdy body and wrinkled face that still seemed kind despite the sorrowful expression. Dube suspected the man was nearly three hundred years old—not unheard of, but definitely elderly.

"Friend or foe?" he asked. It would become the question he and a lot of others asked multiple times each day.

"Neither!" the man spat out. "Just leave me be."

Dube, unwilling to do as the man asked, tried again. "Do you need help? I'm going out to find something to eat. I could get enough for two if I find anything at all, that is."

The stranger chuckled. "You won't find much. I've looked and finally given up. I'm going to sit here until either Cole or Seo comes and takes me."

"How long have you been here? Seo just threatened me yesterday. You can't have been hungry for long."

Actually, it's been weeks since I've had a regular meal or a place to sleep. You see, I was one of Seo's guards while he was in the pit. He talked to me about his plans, and I was so afraid I took off running. I might have been able to stop this war if I had gone to Cole. But I knew Seo's power. And his ability to convince others he was the answer they craved. He had all of the pit under his spell, and I suspected that, when he was released, he would pardon those loyal to him and release them as well. Cole will be no match!"

I heard this exchange and was surprised that this guard was so easily threatened. Did he not understand Cole's power? Did he not know the scriptures? Well, if he didn't, Dube did.

Dube felt sorry for the stranger, "You should come with me. I'm planning on gathering my friends. Hopefully, we will regroup around this cave and hide until this whole thing blows over. You could stay with us. What's your name?"

The stranger hesitated, then scratched himself and burped loudly. He smiled indulgently. "Marc. Mattias Absalom Ruth Caleb in the full. But no, I won't come with you. I'll just sit here. It's all hopeless, you know. But I wish for you, pray for you, to find your people before the end."

Dube was taken aback for a second, but decided he needed to find food and as many of the Boys as possible. Each had to make their own decisions. Free will was Abba's design for mankind. Along with knowing each of them and planning for them to be like Cole.[6] Although no one, least of all Dube, understood.

Dube said goodbye, walked a short way away, then turned to try to convince the stranger one more time to come with him. But there was someone else talking to Marc. Dube thought the new person looked strange, and indeed was. An angel, although Dube couldn't see it at the time. As he watched, the pair walked away from him and slowly disappeared from view. Dube wished Marc well. He knew Marc's despondency firsthand. He was trying with all his might not to succumb at that very moment.

"Let's try to find food, okay?" Well aware that talking to oneself was the first sign of crazy, Dube did it anyway. A one-way conversation was fine until he could find someone else to talk to.

Dube wandered along a dirt track he hoped was leading somewhere. He was amazed at the beauty around him and that it hadn't changed since Seo was released. Shouldn't Abba's creation reflect the terror and despair he was feeling? Instead, the birds were singing, the sky was blue, and the trees and shrubs, green and luscious. Dube looked up into an apple tree and saw all of the fruit there. He didn't know that he had been led there, but he was very grateful for the apples. There was a small basket at the bottom of the tree. Dube looked around to see if anyone had left it, but didn't see another soul.

Dube grabbed a branch just barely within his reach and was thankful for his height like he had never been before. He swung his legs up to rest his feet on the trunk and walked up until he could clamber onto the branch. From there, he climbed up higher until he was in the midst of the apples hanging there. He filled his pockets with the barely pink-blushed green apples. He breathed in the scent of the tree and its fruit and said a small prayer of thanks to Abba and Cole—so maybe he *did* know he was led there! From his mother, he knew to pick the ones that fell off easily into his hands. Anything else could be quite sour. After picking as many as his pockets would hold, Dube worked his way down until he was again on the lowest branch. He was about to drop to the ground when he realized he should survey the surrounding area. He nimbly jumped down and put the apples in his newly acquired basket. Then, he climbed up the tree again to check out the area.

About a half-mile away was a tilled field and a wooden farm-house. The house was painted a cheery white with pink trim and shutters. Despite the morning sunshine, the lights in the house seemed to be on, which made it look even more welcoming. Dube decided to chance going there to see if they had some food they would be willing to share.

Before he got down from the apple tree, Dube surveyed the area around him. He checked for anyone—friend or foe. He became aware that he was using the training he had in swordsmanship classes. At the time, he and Jae often made light of the additional tasks assigned to them. Why bother checking for enemies or finding a good place to hole up or fencing back-to-back to protect each other? The world was at peace. The temple guards held an honorary position, and their only swordplay was in practice to keep their skills sharp. Of course, some of the Bible profs reminded Dube that there would be a war coming, but it seemed unlikely to impossible. "I guess I'm glad Jae and I had that training," he said aloud to no one.

Dube climbed down and headed for the house. I watched him constantly checking his back for anyone or anything that could hurt him and felt sadness at his loss of innocence. But also glad that he was being careful, as it would serve him well.

He reached the house and knocked tentatively. When no one answered after the third try, he turned the doorknob and found the house open. The back door where he entered led directly into the kitchen. The lights were on but were really not necessary. The sunny yellow kitchen was warm and bright with the light from large windows. The spacious square room had counters on all the walls, plenty of space to prepare food for a crowd. In the middle of the space was a heavy, well-used wooden table with ten chairs where the crowd could eat. Dube walked around the perimeter of the room with his hand touching the cool countertops. The action somehow made him feel comforted, no doubt because it reminded him of home. This kitchen was meant for more than food. It was meant for family and friends.

He had been so busy and preoccupied with his thoughts that he didn't realize how hungry he was until he saw the warm bread and butter on the far counter. He picked up a knife to cut a hunk off and saw the note.

"Please, take this bread if you are hungry. There is some dried beef in the upper cabinet and cheese in the fridge. Abba told me someone would come to claim these rations today. Blessings from Him."

Dube should have been surprised, but he wasn't. All morning, he had sensed that Cole and Abba were with him in Spirit and guiding him.

There had been times in his life when Dube had felt he did have a calling. He never told his parents because he was certain it would have made the nagging worse. Plus, he had no real idea what it was. Now, somehow, it felt closer, like something he could almost see out of the corner of his eye. And yet he felt peace even though he didn't understand. He believed his future was tied up in that horrible nightmare, but it no longer bothered him. It would be what it was supposed to be. So no, Dube wasn't surprised that he was led here and there was food prepared and waiting.

What did surprise Dube was when Maj came bounding down the stairs and wrapped him in a bear hug.

CHAPTER 8

Maj

"DUBE! COLE AND ABBA be praised! I'm so glad you're safe."

"Maj! You are indeed a sight for sore eyes! Abba be praised indeed! What are you doing here?"

"Funny you should ask as I was thinking the same thing about you. This is my aunt's house. She passed over just last week, and my family hasn't had time to clear it out or transfer it to another family or even decide what to do. When I ran from the park, I didn't have any idea where to go. I wandered around for a while and actually ran into someone we know. I'll tell you about that in a minute. But finally, it was like a voice in my head said I should come here. I fought it, but it wouldn't let me alone. I even tried to sleep last night in my house, but I dreamed I needed to come here. As soon as I turned the key in the door, I felt peace. I went upstairs and fell into my bed in my bedroom, the one I used when I came to visit my aunt. And I slept peacefully with no more nagging thoughts. Except that I shouldn't lock the doors, and I should bake a loaf of bread and break into my aunt's stash of food. She always had things to feed anyone who came to her door. I felt so safe that I got up this morning and made the bread. And it's for you! I'm so pleased!"

"Not nearly as pleased as I am to have this feast."

Dube and Maj sat at the large table and cut thick slices of the warm bread. They laid out the beef and cheese, and Dube washed and cut up two apples from his basket. Maj said grace, thanking Abba for bringing Dube to her safely and asking for His guidance for them and the rest of the Boys. They ate in relative silence, each thinking about the day before and wondering what came next. But remembering all the miracles that had brought them to this moment, they both gave their anxiety about the "next" to Abba and Cole.

And this was the story of Maj's encounter that she told as they sat full and happy at the table.

After she ran from the park, Maj hid for an hour or so. She found a doorway that had a heavy screen about a foot in front of the door. It was dark in the doorway, so it was difficult for anyone to see Maj, but she could easily see out into the street and hear the conversations going on out there.

"Who is this Dube?" was the most asked question. Apparently, the vid had played on every screen in the world. And the message was startling, so everyone had paid attention. There was so much speculation, so much of it spurious that Maj had the desire many times to jump out and correct the ideas about her lifelong friend. But she was also frightened, so she stayed put.

Until she spotted Tru. He was walking with a very handsome companion who pulled him aside to stop right outside the door where Maj was hiding. They whispered together, then Tru looked straight into the doorway. He was smiling, his eyes crinkling up as though he had just heard something funny or happy. Maj thought, and not for the first time, that Tru was quite good-looking himself.

She opened the screen and stepped onto the sidewalk. Tru immediately pulled Maj into a hug and said, "I'm so glad you're OK! After that awful vid I worried about all of the gang that hung out with Dube."

"Hi, Tru. Thanks! And who's your friend?"

Tru's face darkened, but only for a moment. He pasted on another smile, slightly less welcoming than the first one. "I'm going by Terrance now. And this is Akuma." Akuma picked up Maj's hand and kissed it lightly. "Pleased to meet a friend of Terrance's." There was something disturbing about the gesture. Maj gently removed her hand and said, "Nice to meet you, too."

"Are all of your other friends good? How's Dube?"

"Understandably upset. This Seo character threatened him and actually killed his parents. Who is this guy anyway?"

Tru—I refuse to call him Terrance!—started to speak, but Azuma interrupted. "Seo the Brilliant is the true ruler of this Earth. Abba and Cole imprisoned him unjustly, and Dube's family helped hunt him down when he was hiding. He just got parole and is planning on fighting for his rightful place on the throne of Earth."

Maj was dubious. "'True' ruler? But Cole has been on the throne forever. He is gracious and good to us. Why would Seo want to replace him?"

"Gracious and good?" Akuma spat out. "He's a helicopter parent at best. And a tyrant at worst. You don't have true freedom. You must obey. Seo wants to end all of that. He wasn't given the freedom he craved and was jailed just for wanting it. And telling others about the manipulative ways of Abba. All the way back to Adam and Eve, Seo has been telling Earthers that true freedom and knowledge should belong to them, not solely to Abba. When Seo is ruler, we shall all be truly free to take what we need."

Maj thought about this for a moment. She wasn't a great debater, but felt there was something wrong with this line of reasoning. But then again, she had spent many years studying history to please her parents. And those were useless, wasted years. She did it in part because Abba had said honoring your parents was a good rule. It was one of the Original Ten. Maj had seen a reproduction stone tablet in the Bible Museum where Jae's father and even Jae himself volunteered. Was Cole really a repressive ruler, and she hadn't noticed all of these years as she tried to please Him and her family? Maybe she should listen to what Akuma had to say.

"All right. Tell me more."

Akuma and Tru were inordinately pleased at this. "Let's go have coffee and talk about it. There's a cool place near here where Seo followers hang out. And there's more available than coffee. There are amazing things banned under Cole's rule that can open your mind and help you really see the truth. It's only a few blocks from here. Let's go!"

Maj had lost all of her fear of being out in the open. She felt like Akuma and Tru belonged here in the city, and they would protect her. She sighed happily and set off between them, linking arms with both.

It was not normal that Maj felt this comfortable. Usually, she worried about everything she said and did. Would people like her? Would they approve? But she knew that Tru had been interested in her for many years. He had even asked her out. Why hadn't she accepted? It felt so right now that she stretched up on tiptoes to plant a kiss on Tru's cheek. His real, honest smile returned, making Maj feel special, even tingly. She smiled back.

The trio came to the "cafe" that Akuma had spoken about. They walked in single file as the doorway was rather narrow. Maj had to stop a moment to allow her eyes to adjust to the dark interior. When she could see better, she was amazed at what was there. The walls, ceiling, and floor were painted black, which absorbed most of the light coming from dim lamps with red shades on the scattered tables. There was a space in the middle where some couples were dancing, but to Maj, it appeared they were simply holding each other or groping each other, in no particular rhythm, to the loud music from the stage speakers. There was no band, so she assumed there was a source for the music somewhere. Those who weren't dancing were seemingly enjoying the "amazing things" way too much. Maj had never been one to dodge reality with drugs. She liked being in control. And wasn't that what they said Seo was all about? Controlling your own life and choices. If all these people wanted to avoid whatever was troubling them with mind-altering substances, then Maj was all for it. They could make their own choices, just as she did. She saw that this was a place where young people could escape whatever or whoever was dictating how they should live their lives.

Maj thought over her own choices and how much they had been affected by pleasing her parents, her teachers, and even her peers. Of course, the Boys had been different as they didn't seem to disapprove of anything she did. But that was only four people. Maj craved approval and recognition by, well, basically everyone. She was especially frosted by the lack of contact from Cole. She knew others who had received citizenship or scholarship awards presented to them in ceremonies by the ruler Himself. She longed for everyone to see her in front of the crowds being lauded by the powers that be. She realized she was bitter and angry at the lack of a blessing. Maybe this was a place for her!

She turned to Akuma. "How does a girl get a drink around here?" she said playfully. Akuma's smile in return made her feel warm inside as he said, "Coming right up, beautiful."

A waiter appeared as if by magic at Akuma's elbow, and he whispered in the man's ear, asking for the strongest drink the bartender made. I was frankly worried for Maj as I knew she didn't drink often or much, but I wasn't allowed to interfere. I had to simply watch as the trio made their way to a table in the far corner.

Maj, on the other hand, wasn't worried at all. The warmth of Akuma's attention made her giddy and flirtatious. She thought that she had never been this happy, even when Dube and she had been hanging out with each other. She was always worried about what he thought and frequently gave up her own desires to do what he wanted. Deep in her heart, she knew Dube wouldn't have minded, but the desire to please was too strong in her psyche.

And the first sips of the drinks Akuma had ordered added to the warmth Maj felt and dispelled any lingering anxiety. This was a really good thing! She was so happy to have run into Tru!

And then he spoke.

"Maybe we should go find Dube. Do you know where he is? I know he's upset, but I'm sure Seo would welcome him despite the problems with Dube's parents."

It was like a slap in the face. Maj abruptly stood at the table, knocking over most of the drink in front of her. "You mean their

death? Or was there some other problem you were thinking about?"
she said indignantly. She pushed back the chair and tried to start for
the door, but the dark and loud music was disorienting.

"C'mon, Maj", Akuma said soothingly. "You know it's not like
that. It's about freedom of choice. About not having to please everyone, but being your own person. Making yourself happy. Finding
who you truly are."

All the times Dube had been there for Maj suddenly flooded her
brain. When they played together as kids and Dube would always
let her win at games. When she fell and Dube would usher her back
to the house so Grace could bandage her knees and bring out "me-
dicinal" warm chocolate chip cookies. Grace! Grace and Harald were
dead! Killed by this being Akuma kept saying was good. And Tru was
looking for Dube. Maybe he didn't want her, approve of her, after all.
He only wanted to find Dube so Seo could kill him too. Akuma said
she should be free to choose. She would choose all right! She would
choose Dube. And Cole. And Abba.

"I don't like it here. I'm going."

"Don't go yet. We really like you and want you to stay." Suddenly,
Akuma's tone became menacing, even though the words were not.
And it was like he knew how to sway Maj. Tell her she pleased them
and they liked her. Or threaten her when she didn't comply.

Maj felt a warm hand at the small of her back. "Let's get out of
here," the voice said. She instantly turned and followed the stranger
out the door, with Akuma and Tru calling after her, seemingly more
insistent and desperate the farther she was from them. And just as
she exited the cafe, she heard Akuma say, "Come back, Terrance.
She's not worth it. We'll find him another way."

So, Tru had only sweet-talked to get her to betray Dube! The stranger had rescued her from their "nefarious" plans. She laughed at the word Jae had used, and became aware of how much she missed all of the Boys. She turned to thank the stranger, but he was gone. Him? Why did she think it was a man?

"And you know the rest, Dube," Maj said as she finished telling her tale. "So, we need to find the other Boys to make sure they aren't fooled like I almost was."

And just like that, Gaz walked through the door. But he wasn't alone. Sim was with him.

Gaz

THERE WAS MUCH HUGGING and happy tears and introductions. Maj offered food and drink as the pair seemed like they had been traveling a while. And they had.

When Gaz left the park, he wandered around Nusan for a few hours. There was little to show the great change that had just happened. Every now and again there would be a house or business building where the door was open or broken down or the whole building had burned. Those places were sobering and Gaz tried not to imagine what had occurred there. It was bad enough to have the images of Grace and Harald to contend with, so he hurried past.

Gaz kept walking, looking for any of the Boys or anyone he knew. He felt like he needed the comfort of familiarity. While he was still blocks away from U Square, he heard music and voices. He picked up his pace and, when the Square came into view, he stopped for a second in awe. Here was the center of the action. There were hundreds of people dancing with abandon to a live band. Many of them were throwing off clothes and writhing in various states of undress, despite the coolness of the day. There was kissing, hugging, and groping among the dancers. Some people appeared to be having sex right there in the midst of the crowd. Gaz lowered his eyes and blushed. The music was intoxicating and Gaz found himself wanting to join the crowd. He even started to remove his shirt. But when the cold breeze off the bay hit his chest, it revived his senses as if someone had thrown a glass of ice water in his face. He shook his head to clear the cobwebs and buttoned up again. He turned away from the Square and started to walk. Then he started to run. He kept on running until the music was gone and the images of the crowd began to fade.

Gaz ran until he came to the ancient Sanctuary known as Grace. And here he experienced the shock he was trying to avoid all morning. The door was broken in and the place smelled of smoke and ash. The interior was blackened and the roof had fallen in. All of the lovely stained glass was broken in tiny shards around the outside walls, looking as though there was a violent explosion that had blown the windows out. He could look through the door but there was too much debris to go inside. This place was sacred, despite a somewhat patchy history prior to TE. Gaz was aghast that anyone would destroy it. He thought of the Temple in Jerusalem and quickly prayed that Abba and the guards had protected it. *Didn't Dube and Jae talk about becoming Temple guards? I can tell you they had. What ever became of that? And where was Dube anyway? Was he safe?*

The anxiety of not knowing was bothering Gaz and he felt the irresistible pull of comfort. And, at this moment, the most comfortable place he could think of was Soasind. Specifically, Nuchen, where his parents had grown up and he still had many relatives. Was it only this morning that he had vized back from there and broken his arranged engagement? It seemed like forever.

There was a vizport a block away that Gaz knew about and he hoped it was undamaged. As he approached, he noticed there were some odd beings that appeared to be guarding the port. They were not Hume but seemed to have the same general bodily characteristics. Except they had wings, and one of them had three pairs of them. They were somehow attractive and repulsive at the same time. Gaz couldn't stop staring. He was thankful that he had seen them; but, so far, they hadn't seen him. The word *"demon"* came to his mind unbidden, but he wasn't sure that was right. After all, no one had seen a demon for a thousand years. They were mentioned in scripture, but hadn't they been cast into the Pit with Seo?[7] And then he remembered that Seo was loose. And it all suddenly made sense. The damage to the Sanctuary, Grace and Harald's death, the wild *"orgy"*—another unbidden word—in the Square. He almost laughed with joy at the understanding, until he realized the horror of it all.

But right now, Gaz needed to find a way to get rid of those guards so he could viz home. A plan formed in his mind. He quickly understood that it was pure nonsense. But the desire to go was so strong he thought he might as well die trying. He was going to walk toward the beings and ask to use the vizport.

He approached the port, and the demons turned to face him. One of them raised an arm in greeting and said, "Seo is King." Gaz quickly thought and replied, "And Ruler of Earth." He was surprised at the words that came out, but the demons only smiled. Of course, Gaz knew that Cole was the actual Ruler, but somehow, he thought of the scriptures where Seo had been proud and tried to overthrow Abba.[8] He knew Seo believed he was the true ruler. Apparently, the demons also believed.

"What can we do for you, Follower?"

"I'd like to use the port if it's working. I want to tell my extended family the news and invite them to join me here for the celebrations. Is that possible?"

"Sure! We can unlock and program the port. Would you like a round-trip viz?"

Gaz smiled at his ability to fool these beings. They, of course, thought he was happy at the thought of celebrating Seo's inevitable victory. "Yes, please! The 'Ruler' is generous and, I'm sure, would be pleased at your good service. I'll be bringing back others, so it will need to be a multi-viz."

"Certainly! The Morning Star be praised!"

"The Son of the Dawn is worthy." It was all Gaz could do to keep from recoiling at those disgusting words. But it would all be worth it to see his family again. He paused as the demons programmed the vizport and then stepped gingerly into it, waved goodbye to them, and included a quick, unseen rude hand gesture as he disappeared from their view.

The sights and smells of his parents' homeland immediately soothed Gaz's troubled soul. He always resisted coming here for visits. Resisted his parents' guidance and planning for him. Resisted the arranged marriage. In his sorrow and doubt about what to do next, he regretted all of the fighting and stubbornness.

As Gaz made his way to his Nani and Dadi's house, he passed by a virtual dichotomy of gatherings. There were the wild street parties of Seo and his followers—although in this conservative culture the celebrations were generally clothed and sexless. The groups loyal to Abba and Cole tended to be in houses whispering about plans or sorrowing about anyone who had been taken or killed. As Gaz walked along the dusty paths—so different from the green of Nusan—he wondered at the two camps that Seo's release had engendered. Before this, it seemed that there had been only one group that was loyal to Cole and His father Abba. It puzzled Gaz how those who had lived in the peace and care of the Ruler could now turn against Him. Another word came to Gaz. *Rebellion.* An open resistance to the established rule or government. Was that what Gaz had been doing his entire life: resisting, rebelling?

His thoughts were interrupted by the smells of naan cooking in an outdoor oven. A vendor. He realized it had been a long time since he had eaten naan and the smell of the bread was making him salivate. Gaz searched his pockets for his kudo card. Although everything was free in Cole's kingdom, people still "paid" vendors and service people with a tangible thanks to say they were pleased. These accolades were stored up and, once a year at the Praise festival, were presented to Cole as a way to acknowledge that everything came from Him.

As he passed the card to the vendor, the man sneered. "That's no good here, son. Cole never did a thing for me. I'm putting my money on Seo and looking forward to the freedom his rule will give me. Take your naan and be on your way. Seo still wants all food to be free to his people. I hope you will join us."

Gaz walked away from the stall, munching the warm bread and wondering again about this newly released being. *Who was he, and what did he stand for?* It seemed he had encouraged some to be killed, but there were many who thought his ways were better and were willing to follow him. He shook his head for what seemed to be the millionth time today in wonder.

And then a sight caught his eyes. It was Sim's house, his intended fiancée. The house was in ruins, blackened by fire, with the roof caved in and debris everywhere. Well, almost everywhere. Weirdly, there was one corner of the structure standing. It had a separate entrance on the side, and its two floors were clean and complete—all four walls were there as if it were a separate, single-room, double-story dwelling. Gaz carefully and quietly made his way into the odd structure.

Just like most of the houses in this area it was made of teak wood with thick glass windows to keep out the heat. All new building on Earth was made of natural materials now. Yes, there were still structures that had survived the first Event and were less natural, like Grace Cathedral. Gaz shuddered as he remembered the destruction there. But new buildings were less toxic and more beautiful, in almost everyone's opinion. As was this house. At least the part that was standing.

Gaz blinked as the interior was currently unlit. He tried the switch that energized the bioluminescent fixtures, but he failed to turn them on. He closed his eyes for a minute to allow them to adjust to the dark. He was in a dressing room. Many houses had dressing rooms on the first floor that accompanied the bedrooms on the second. There were old-fashioned, brightly-colored saris everywhere—a few hanging up in the closet, some draped across the chairs and desk, and most on the floor. Many had gold or silver embroidery at the hems. Whoever was the resident of these rooms apparently loved beautiful clothes and hated neatness. Gaz chuckled to himself. This place reminded him of his rooms back in the city. With less silk and embroidery, of course.

Then Gaz remembered that Sim had loved dressing up in trad. Before he had nixed their union, she had breathlessly told him about the wedding she envisioned, with many changes of clothes and days of celebration. It was one of the things that had made up his mind to end it. Now he wondered if he had acted rashly. Like usual.

Then the thought that this might actually be Sim's rooms spurred him to action. He saw the stair to the bedroom above and ran up it. This room was lighter as it had many more windows to take advantage of the view and fresh air in the winter months. He scanned the room quickly and saw a figure sprawled across the sleeping mats. It was Sim.

Gaz started to weep as he realized Sim and her family had been killed. He knew they were fiercely loyal to Cole and imagined that was why the house was in ruins and the family gone. Or mostly gone. Here was Sim's body for some reason. Gaz was determined to get her out of here and give her a proper burial—or whatever would pass for a funeral as the conflict escalated. He made his way over to the mat and sat down beside SIm. "I'm so sorry. Really, about everything. Maybe I should have considered marrying you. I don't know. What will it all matter now?"

Gaz wiped his tears and gently kissed Sim's cheek. He gasped as she opened her eyes, "You're alive!"

Sim smiled gently, then kissed him back, more passionately this time, and on the lips. "I was only asleep. It's a good thing you didn't want to become a doctor."

'Wha—wha—what happened here?" he stammered out.

"Oh, Gaz, it was incredible! Seo came and freed me! You know my parents were so strict and wanted to control my life. I just wanted to make my own choices. They kept me locked up and made me dress in silky saris and slippers that would barely stay on my feet! I wanted to put on shorts and tees and boots and go out hiking! But that wasn't 'ladylike.' I had to be a china doll, dressed up to fulfill my parents' fantasies of the good daughter. I'm sad that they are gone, but more than that, I'm delirious that I'm finally free! I threw that glitter and finery all around my dressing room downstairs and pulled out my favorite clothes that I had to keep hidden!"

Gaz was stunned, but managed a *"Yes, I saw that"* reply.

Sim continued. "I am so glad you broke our engagement! I know you want a traditional girl. I'm not that. You'll find someone under Seo's reign. He will let you choose whatever makes you happy. There won't be restrictions or the Registry. You can try out anyone you feel attracted to, and if you're not sexually compatible, you can move on to someone else. The freedom he will allow us all to have. Seo is King!"

"And Ruler of Earth." Gaz was stunned. The phrase came naturally to his lips. Was this what he actually felt? Sim was right about a few things. And wrong about others. He decided to set her straight.

"You don't know me, Sim. Don't think you understand me. My parents always did that, and I hated it. I want to choose what I do with my life! I want to choose my partner or choose not to have one at all. Why should I settle into the life my parents had? A nice house, a wife, two-and-a-half kids—that was the dream before the Event. My friends, the Boys, all want to postpone our choice-of-life path. Or not pursue a Purpose at all! Why can't we just keep on hanging out, playing Frisbee and chilling? We're only thirty! We most likely will live to be a couple of hundred years old. Some live even longer. Why do we need to commit to a job and life goals now? You're right. We need the freedom to choose. Cole used to say we had freedom of choice, but we didn't really, did we?"

Sim looked at Gaz for a long moment. It was like she was seeing him for the first time. Even though they had grown up together and spent many hours lately under the watchful eyes of chaperones "getting to know one another." She had an irresistible urge to kiss him again. To get to know him physically. She lay back on the mat and pulled Gaz down on top of her.

"Wait," he protested slightly, but his body told her that the reticence wouldn't last long. Gaz kissed Sim's forehead, her cheeks, her soft lips. It appeared they were going to see if they were sexually compatible.

I looked away.

They eventually fell asleep.

When they woke up the next morning, they both felt a happiness they had never experienced before. Happiness, but not joy. Not the deep feeling that a relationship with Abba gave rise to, no matter the circumstances. But they had been right about one thing. Abba gave Hume freedom to choose. And they had chosen. I wept.

Gaz and Sim got dressed, she in shorts and boots.

Gaz wanted to share his happiness with the Boys, the ones who mattered most to him in the world. He remembered the cave and had some vague recollection that this was a place to gather if the Boys ever got separated. Maybe they would all be there!

Gaz and Sim made their way to the nearest vizport. This time he didn't have to scheme and pretend. He really believed that Seo was king and ruler. He could answer the demon guards with conviction.

They got out of the vizport in a small town center. Gaz had a memory of Maj and her aunt hosting his family one weekend and he and his brother coming here for groceries. Yes, there was the market where they had shopped. And he knew the cave was close to Maj's aunt's house. He decided to stop by the house on the way to the cave to see if Maj's aunt would give him some food and drink to take to the cave. If not, he would simply take it. It was his right under Seo. They would soon be celebrating with their friends.

Of course, that's not what happened.

Gaz was surprised to see his friends there, but happy too. He reported all that had happened to him in the day and a half since they have been together in the park. He finished by saying, "And Sim and I made love," which made Maj blush and Sim look triumphant. Gaz continued, "I don't understand why Cole would deny us this pleasure! We should be free to have sex whenever and with whoever pleases us."

Dube looked at his friend with concern. "Gaz, you're using Abba's grace to abuse His grace."

For the second time in two days, Gaz was stunned, almost speechless. His dearest friends didn't understand. They weren't happy for him. Gaz's rebellious nature reared its head in full force. When he finally spoke, it was piercing. "I thought you of all people would understand. Your strict parents are gone, thanks to Seo. You can do and be anything you want. Or nothing at all. You should be happy for me, for us! Stop parroting what Cole says and be your own man!"

Dube was about to reply but Maj beat him to it. She always wanted to please people, and she had nearly infinite patience with foolishness and bad behavior. She always tried to diffuse anger

GAZ

and conflict with kind words or consolation. But not this time. She walked right up to Gaz with a steely look in her eyes. She barely came up to his chin, but her demeanor made Gaz take a step back. "Get out of my house." The words were not loud, but there was no doubt about the meaning. She was often described by her friends as "tiny but dangerous."

Gaz looked stunned for a moment, then grabbed Sim by the hand and quickly left without another word.

Maj then grabbed Dube by the hand and took him into the living room where she knelt on the soft rug. Dube knelt beside her, understanding immediately that Maj was going to talk to their Father. They cried together for a minute, then they prayed. They prayed for Dube's parents; they prayed for Gaz and Sim to come back to the truth. They thanked the Father for showing them the way.

CHAPTER 10

Vel

IF THEY HAD KNOWN what happened to Vel, they would have prayed for her as well.

Vel ran as fast as she could from the park. And she could run. In addition to just scattering as the group had suggested to protect Dube, Vel found that running freed her mind and calmed her fears. It had always been that way. Her tendency to speak without filters had garnered a lot of trouble over the years. And made it hard for her to find and keep friends. The Boys were different in that regard. They often helped her to see how her comments could hurt others, but never rejected her. She let herself relax with them.

Running, however, was where she felt safe and powerful and never embarrassed. Maybe it was in part because she generally didn't speak while she ran.

So, leaving the park, she ran and kept running, until her legs ached and her labored breathing couldn't supply her muscles with enough oxygen to keep running. She slowed to a walk. She had run across the bridge and was in the city of Oak. As she crossed the bridge, the sun sparkled on the water, the wind whipping up tiny wavelets with foam headdresses. But Vel noticed none of that.

She eventually reached the hills of Oak, which made it harder to keep going. So she stopped. She sat down on a bench in a park and rested, closing her eyes. The birdsong and gentle rustle of leaves relaxed her, and her breathing became slower as her body recharged.

One of the reasons Vel had run across the bridge to Oak was because she had history here. She had started Uni here before transferring to the school where she met Dube and Gaz.

Vel's parents still lived here as well. And that was where she headed now. The Boys accepted Vel for who she was, no provisos. Her parents accepted her in a different way. They saw her potential and pushed her to achieve. They didn't criticize her for falling short, but they didn't allow her to quit either. They kept encouraging, cheering her successes and lamenting her failures for a second or two before telling her to try again, that this time she would win. Winning was important to Vel's parents.

Vel saw the familiar outline of her childhood home. It was a large, three-story stone house, basically a mansion, situated on a prime hill with a view of Nusan Bay. The warm yellow stone always made Vel think of sunshine, although it was more butter-colored. She breathed a sigh of relief that her house was standing as she had passed many houses and businesses that were burned or hollowed out. There were lights on in the upper story which was comforting as it was late afternoon and the sunlight was beginning to dim.

As Vel approached the house she heard what sounded like a party. She wasn't surprised about the gathering, but was taken aback as it seemed a celebration. Considering what had just happened to Dube's family she thought the mood might be more somber. Well, nothing to do but investigate.

She approached the house and took the stone path to the side of the structure that led to the gate. She opened the gate slowly as she knew the hinges squeaked. She needn't have bothered. The noise was coming from the back deck and was loud enough to drown out cannon fire. Vel was still cautious in case this party was none of her parents' doing. She moved furtively, almost on tiptoes, toward the back of the house. As she peeked around the corner, she saw a very large group gathered in the backyard. No one seemed to notice her so she took a moment to survey the situation.

There were knots of people talking, but there also seemed to be a dance floor of tiles that had been constructed on the lawn below the deck. People were "dancing," but as Maj had noticed in the club and Gaz at the square, there was more than dancing happening here. Beyond the dancers at the bottom of the yard was an odd contraption of tubes and tubs with clear bottles of liquid on a table nearby. Vel recognized this apparatus, weirdly from one of the Old Earth films that Dube's parents had in their collection. It was a *still*. Something to distill alcohol from grain mash or grape mash. Just for a moment, Vel felt the hurt of Dube's parents' death. Then her attention was brought back to the present and the still. Wine was allowed, but hard alcohol was not permitted in Cole's kingdom! She was shocked, first of all, that her parents had allowed it, and, secondly, that Cole hadn't yet destroyed it and punished them. And then she remembered that Seo had been loosed and evil was back in the world. Apparently, it was fueled by large amounts of liquor.

Vel searched the crowd for anyone she knew. She was in the midst of a multitude and had never felt so lonely in her life. She longed to see one of the Boys but knew in her heart they would never be involved in such a carnal gathering. Then she saw her mother, the center of attention in a small cluster of people. She let out a breath she hadn't realized she was holding. "Mom!" she cried and ran through the crowd to give her mother a hug, but she was stopped short as her mother grabbed her and kept her at arm's length. Vel was shocked. They weren't an overly demonstrative or mushy family, but she had never been denied the comfort of her parents' embrace. She stepped back.

"Hi, honey. What are you doing back from the city? No classes today? No matter! I'm so glad you're here instead of with those losers." The group around Vel's mother chuckled at the judgment.

Vel wasn't sure how to answer. She felt like she needed to hold her breath again, like she needed to be cautious. This was a totally new experience for her. She quickly thought of something to say.

"There was a lot going on in the city and I needed to come home and check that you and Dad are all right."

"Of course, we are! We met a bunch of new friends today and decided to throw a party to welcome them."

"Oh, okay."

"Come meet some people. Everyone, this is our daughter, Vel. She's an extremely talented athlete, takes after her father and me of course!" Her mother giggled. Giggled like a silly child! Vel had never heard such a thing from her competitive, no-nonsense mother. She needed to regroup.

But her mother grabbed Vel's arm and started to show her around to the various cliques that formed the party. The music and the insensibility of it all began to make Vel dizzy, and as soon as she was able to pry her arm out of her mother's grasp, she moved away and sat on a bench near the back of the yard. Her mother hardly noticed and continued to hold court with the partygoers who thronged around her. She knew her mother liked having everyone's attention and admiration, but this seemed to be carrying that a bit far.

It was quieter where Vel sat, and she thought about her friends back in the city. She hoped they were all right. As she mused about the Boys, a beautiful creature approached her with a glass of wine. While she seemed to be a woman, there was definitely something different about her.

"Here," she said, "you look like you need this. Didn't expect an invasion when you came home?" The last was said with a slight smile of amusement.

The lightness of the remark made Vel realize how angry she was. "No, I didn't! Who are all of these jerks anyway?"

The woman sat beside Vel and looked deep into her eyes. "I'm so sorry we upset you. We're a group that has views similar to your parents' and we came to encourage them to become leaders and examples. We know conflict is coming, and we wanted to recruit them as soon as possible. Not only were they amenable but they decided to throw a party and invite others to hear as well."

"Well, I've had a horrible day, and I'm not in the mood for politics! I just wanted to come home. But maybe I should be going."

"Oh, no! Don't go, please. You seem like a person who says exactly what they mean. We really need you too! Maybe even more than your parents. They can be figureheads, but you could be the substance of our movement. We're encouraging freedom and choice, more than the current leadership allows. We need straight talk like you've just demonstrated. Can we go into your house and speak further, away from the noise and frivolity?"

"Okay. But why not just break up the frivolity if you think it's useless? If these people are worthless?" Vel winced as she heard the words come from her mouth. These were the kind of things she used to say all the time. The things she would be punished or scolded for. But the stranger didn't seem to mind at all.

"Freedom, remember? This is what some want, and our leader is willing to let them have that. But you are destined for greater things."

Vel was intrigued. Here was someone who valued her "no filters" speech. *Was this too good to be true?*

The woman continued. "I'm sure you think I'm just flattering you, but I'm not. We came to this house knowing your parents were here, but praying you would come home. The leader has followed your life and choices and is impressed by your willingness to call things as they are. You don't hesitate to speak when you see stupidity or ridiculous behavior. You laugh at convention. You deride the status quo if it makes no sense. We love your attitude."

Vel blushed ever so slightly. Even her unusually light complexion didn't hint at the embarrassment she felt. Then she quickly banished the feeling. *Why shouldn't her directness be celebrated? Who was this stranger? And what was this movement she hadn't yet heard about?*

"I'm Blake. Let me tell you about us and our great Leader."

Vel was struck by the fact that Blake answered the questions rolling around in her head without her having to ask. But this thought was also banished quickly as Vel felt a peace about the path she saw before her. So much of her life had been fighting her natural inclination to speak before thinking. The "gumball effect," Grace had called it. Well, who was Grace to criticize her?! (I can tell you there wasn't any criticism in the comment, but merely observation.) Surely, this peace was Abba telling her this was the path she was always meant to take. That His gift of forthright speech was now to be not the burden it had been in the past but a true gift and a way to help others see the right path. She smiled at Blake and took her proffered arm.

"Let's go up to my room and talk some more. I think I like what you're saying, and I like you. Let me hear more about how much you value me and my frank speech."

Blake smiled sweetly. At least that's what Vel thought. I thought it looked a bit menacing. And I was not at all comforted by Blake grabbing a full bottle of the clear liquor and two glasses as she followed Vel to the stairs.

CHAPTER 11

Jae

AT LEAST JAE HAD chosen well. Actually, he had chosen what was better.[9]

When Jae left the park, he walked quickly away and into the surrounding neighborhood. He was not the athlete that Vel was and didn't have Dube's long, loping gait. He walked as fast as possible and prayed as he did. He was not only stunned by the vid but worried about Dube. His best friend for what he considered to be his entire life had just lost the two most important people in his life. Of course, Dube would never say that. He would tell you how irritating his folks were, how they constantly nagged, and how weird their old ways were. But Jae knew. He saw the love between them and knew now that Dube would miss them terribly.

Parents! If Dube's parents were in trouble, surely his family was in danger too! His father was openly loyal to Cole and Abba. Dr. Pac listened as his students debated the Ruler's control over the Earth and the good and bad—as the students saw it—that they said were the results. Old Earth rulers had many restraints placed on them by their subjects, as they were humans with a sin nature. And power corrupted. But there was no bad, no corruption in Cole. He ruled as He saw fit with no constraints. And Dr. Pac patiently told his students that.

His father had told Jae many times about Seo and his imprisonment, and how at some point he would be let out. He wanted Jae to be prepared to see that some would follow Seo, despite the long, prosperous, and conflict-free reign of Cole. Jae had listened only with half attention, but now the lectures came back to him like a brain flood. *Some would follow. They would choose Seo over their Savior. But why?*

Jae hurried to his house on the opposite side of the city from the park. He also passed some houses and buildings that were ransacked or burned. His treasured clothing store with the funky sayings T-shirts he favored. Gone. The small grocery store was standing but looked like there had been a run on food. He waved at the owner as he hurried by. The man looked overwhelmed, but Jae didn't have time to help him. Perhaps he would come back. But now the desire to see how his parents were overrode any other thoughts.

As Jae turned down his street, he saw that his house was also damaged. Like Dube, Jae's parents had lived in an Old Earth dwelling that was for his family alone. The beautiful wood door was hanging half off the hinges. There was no hint of the dark green paint of the window sashes and doors, or the soft coral of the stucco. Everything was black. Jae was worried but not yet dismayed. He carefully picked his way around the debris and entered the front door. He made his way back to the kitchen where every dish, every pot, pan, and cooking implement had been smashed on the floor. He stepped gingerly over to the walk-in "freezer" that was still closed with the numeric lock. He entered his parents' wedding date—and slightly rolled his eyes at the romance of it—and the door swung open. He stepped into a small landing preceding a staircase heading down. He closed the door behind him to keep anyone else from entering and started down the staircase.

At the bottom of the stairs, there was a living room. His parents sat on the sofa reading. Jae had never seen such a welcome sight in his entire life. He took a moment to thank Abba, gathered and calmed himself as he knew his parents would expect, and said, "So, I see the panic apartment came in handy."

Despite what he thought would happen, his parents exclaimed with joy, threw their books aside—sacrilege for a professor!— and ran to Jae to enclose him in a hug. And he didn't mind in the least.

His father had spent many hours building this place with Jae and a few trusted friends. He knew what was coming and wanted a safe enclave for his family and others. Dr. Pac knew some needed to fight. But he also knew that some would need rest or regrouping, and he thought Cole wanted him to plan for that.

"How are you, son? We saw the 'execution' of Dube's parents and were worried about all of you."

"I'm fine, Dad. Or as fine as I can be considering they were just murdered before our eyes." Jae stopped a moment to consider what he had just heard. "Why did you say 'execution' in that tone?"

"Actually, son, they weren't killed. Cole took them up, just like Elijah[10], before the bullets found their mark. Cole told me himself so there is no doubt."

Jae was awestruck. "You spoke to Cole?" Then the hint of a smile crossed his lips as he said, "And you weren't being disciplined?" Jae knew his father would never do anything against Cole and Abba. He loved Them and the Word too much. Pac just shook his head and smiled back at his son.

The rest of the afternoon passed peacefully as father and son discussed what Revelation said and its implications. The discussion was interrupted a few times as the signal doorbell rang and family and friends requested to come into the safety of the apartment. There was plenty of room for all and lots of lively discussion, followed by some leaving to carry out the work they knew they needed to do.

It was very late when Jae and his father had exhausted themselves in thought and word. Jae had a second bedroom in the apartment and his father encouraged him to rest and let their discussion fill his dreams before deciding what to do next. Dr. Pac was very wise and his son was smart enough to know that.

And fill his dreams it did. It was honestly surprising that Jae was rested the next morning considering all of the wild, scary, and just weird visions that occupied his night. But the next morning he knew exactly what the next step was, and he was at peace that the step after that and the step after that would be revealed to him when the time was right.

He dressed and went to the kitchen, where the enthusiastic debates continued. Jae was getting anxious being around so many people and so much talk. He made himself a sandwich of sausage, cheese, and bread and packed a pear into his already prepared backpack. He had packed some extra clothes, a warm blanket in case he had to sleep rough, and his sword. The short sword, of course, since the long blade would have cleaved the pack in two. He kissed his mother and hugged his father and told them not to worry. He was certain he would be fine, no matter what happened.

Jae climbed the stairs and left the noise and crowd behind. He carefully closed the door to the apartment, then arranged a bunch of broken and burned rubble in front of it to hide the fact that it had been opened. "Go with God," he said to no one there, but everyone below him in the sanctuary.

Jae looked right and left and exited the house cautiously, but then ambled along through the city like he belonged there. He knew not to hurry or look afraid as it would draw attention to him. He kept walking until he was on the outskirts of town. After he left the last of the city buildings, there were meadows and copses of trees. He walked along, relaxed now as he was definitely alone. The air and grass were still damp from the overnight mist that watered the Earth. He marveled, not for the first time and certainly not for the last, that Abba had created something breathtaking.

Jae made his way to the cave. When he was at the mouth he called out, "Anyone there?" and was disappointed by the lack of an answer. He knew beyond doubt that this was where he was supposed to go. But he had hoped to find Dube waiting.

As he entered the cave he tensed, seeing that he was not alone any longer. There was a table set and water to drink in crystal glasses. It was actually a flat rock covered by a beautiful silver cloth, but it was impressive for a cave in the middle of nowhere. He stopped and looked around, then reached into his pack to grasp the handle of his sword. He stepped beyond the table to venture further into the cave and saw a man sitting on a rock. At least, that's what Jae thought at first. He greeted the person, hoping that this wasn't going to turn into a fight as the cave was a bit of a tight space for swinging a blade.

"Let go of the sword, Jae. I'm not going to harm you. I'm here to tell you about the battle that will start soon, and your part in it. Be not afraid."

And with the last words Jae's eyes were opened and he realized that he was talking to Cole himself. He threw the backpack aside and fell on his face.

"I'm not worthy, Christ Our Lord Eternal!"

"Rise, honored son of Pac and Ela. You and the Boys have a part to play in this, the last battle."

"You know about the Boys? Oh, sorry, what a stupid question! Omniscient, of course! My father would smack me upside the head if he were here. Oh! What am I saying to the Ruler of the Earth, the Savior of all men, the Lamb of God? Sorry again! I'll shut up now."

To his amazement, Cole started chuckling, then laughing, then practically roaring with mirth at Jae. "You, my child, are a welcome respite from all of the horrors and evil that has been loosed on the Earth. Come, sit with me and we'll talk."

And Jae listened, asking occasional questions for the rest of the day. He was so grateful to be in the Lord's presence like this that the hours flew by. He had never felt so loved, even with his deeply loving parents. He had never felt so seen and understood. He never wanted to leave, even though he knew in his heart that this was only for a time.

Food appeared on the table when he needed to eat and eventually it grew dark outside the cave. He struggled to keep his eyes open and hear more of what Cole had to say. But the time came when he needed to sleep. There was a bed made up in a corner and the cave was warm. As he climbed under the covers, he thanked Cole one more time.

"We will honor you, Most High God. There are not words to say how much today has meant to me, and I know the Boys will be beyond grateful that you have chosen us."

"Sleep, my child. Tomorrow will come soon."

Jae closed his eyes and immediately fell into a restful sleep. All of the strange dreams of the previous night were gone.

CHAPTER 12

The Boys

THE NEXT MORNING JAE woke. He saw that the cave was completely empty now, the table once again a rock. Cole had told him where to go, so he packed up his things, taking the extra blanket from the bed, and set out for the farmhouse. He passed the apple tree as he walked but didn't stop to gather fruit. In almost no time he was at the farmhouse door and decided he should just walk right in.

When Dube saw his best friend after two days apart he jumped up from the breakfast that he and Maj had prepared, jostling the table as he did, and ran to hug Jae and playfully kiss him on both cheeks.

"Get off, you weirdo!" Jae laughed. But, of course, he didn't mean it. He was just as happy as Dube and embraced him back. Maj just grinned.

"Where are Gaz and Vel?"

"I'm sorry, Jae. Gaz decided to abandon Cole. He found Sim, his former fiancée, and decided that Seo's plan was what he wanted. His rebellion has taken him to a very bad place, but we couldn't talk him out of it. I'm crushed. And Vel just disappeared. I'm assuming the worst for her as well, but we will know someday, and just maybe she is good."

Jae took a moment to feel the losses, but only a moment. He knew that they needed to start out soon. He decided that diving right in was the best policy.

"I have news and instructions from Cole. We are most blessed to be part of His plan."

"Did you dream what Cole wanted us to do?" Dube asked. He knew that Jae occasionally had dreams or visions. They would check them against the Word, or consult Dr. Pac or another wise elder, to make sure they were consistent with Cole's teachings, then proceed either to carry them out or discard them.

Jae looked shy for a moment. He was honored that Cole had spoken to him, but he had been told that Dube was the blessed one. Jae didn't mind, but wanted to be careful not to be proud of the fact that he had been at Cole's feet.

"Actually, I went to our cave, and He was there. We spoke about the plans all day yesterday. I am beyond blessed that I received His words, but you are the one chosen to lead. The final battle will be nothing. Seo doesn't understand that he is not powerful compared to Abba. He thinks he will win. But when he gets to Jerusalem, he will be destroyed by fire. We, however, have been given the task of clearing the Registry vizport here in Nusan. Once that is done, all of the Registry ports around the world will be open. Anyone who wants to go to Jerusalem for the final battle will have access, no matter which side they are on. But the people and demons guarding the port here need to be defeated. And they will be, Cole assured me. We need to leave soon, basically right now."

Dube was stunned. Beyond stunned. He was supposed to lead in a battle? Sure, he was top of his class in swordsmanship, but he was only one. Okay, Jae was close to his level of expertise, so they were only two. He was certain that Maj could handle a sword, but not anywhere near their ability. So, two and a half. Dube got distracted by his thoughts for a moment as they were always calling Maj "a half." Then he realized how serious this was.

"Me and what army? And even if I had an army, I couldn't lead them. I mean, why would they follow me? I'm not a great motivator. I'm not qualified to do this!"

Maj looked from Jae to Dube and back again, expecting Jae to answer the objections. But he just lowered his eyes and looked a bit disappointed. *"Okay,"* Maj thought. *"I guess it's up to me."*

She walked up to Dube, just like she had the day before with Gaz, and faced him squarely. Dube didn't back up because he knew Maj loved him. He thought she was going to tell him it was fine and that there would be someone else qualified to lead who would step forward. Instead, she said, "Daniel Uzziah Benjamin Ezekial! Stop channeling Moses! Cole and Abba have called you! You, the least of men, to lead because he chooses foolishness to confound the wise![11] Abba will provide the army. And if he doesn't, we three will be enough. Think about Gideon. Think about David defeating the giant. Even Moses, once he stopped whining, experienced God's power. You aren't enough, it's true. But He is."

Now Dube stepped back. *Could it really be true?* He had no way to verify what Jae said except he trusted Jae completely. He remembered his mother's words about faith and action. *There were times,* she had said, *that you just needed to start moving in a direction and trust Abba to turn you or stop you if need be.* The first step might be the hardest.

But why should he take Jae's word that this was Cole's mission? He loved his friend but his visions did sometimes turn out to be anything between foolish and dangerous. And why the rush? Let him think about it a while, pray over it, read scripture, and study what he should do. Surely the decision of his life's purpose wasn't meant to be taken lightly and rushed into. If this even was his life's purpose.

And then his thought became clear, like the fog lifting off Nusan Bay. The nightmare that repeated ad nauseam. His inability to choose a path because the path wasn't ready for him yet. Grace and Harald's faith in him that he was destined. They never said *for what*, just that *he was*. So, this must be it, his Purpose.

Might as well not delay.

"All right. Let's get our swords and go back into the city. I love and trust you both, so even if we die, we'll do it together. For Cole and Abba."

Without another word, the three knelt down, said a quick prayer for protection and guidance, and set out.

Just as they were walking toward the kitchen door, they heard a knock. They each drew their swords without speaking or checking what the others did. Maj figured she was the most expendable of the trio, so she moved toward the door, grabbed the handle, and opened it. To everyone's amazement, Esther was standing on the stoop, and there was a small group of others behind her. Most with swords.

"Hi! Maj, isn't it? Someone in the group had a vision that we should come here to find Dube. Is he here?"

Jae moved forward and kissed Esther on the cheek. Whatever had happened in the past was well over, or had been a mutual decision. They were obviously both happy with the relationship they had now.

"I'm here," Dube said as he stepped forward.

Esther drew him into a hug. "I have a vid for you to watch. This was given to us by a spy in Seo's troops. It concerns your parents."

Maj riffled through some cabinets in the living room and found a device that would play the vid. The group with Esther had seen it, so they let the three friends watch it together. Jae held both Maj and Dube's hands as they watched Grace and Harald face their death. And then they disappeared. And the guards and followers erupted in swearing and foul tempers as they threw aside the clothing on the ground, searching through it as if they could find the pair underneath. Jae chuckled a bit, then stopped himself and said, "I'm sorry."

Dube looked up with tears in his eyes. "No, my friend, you are right. It's hilarious. Mom and Dad were taken. I've never seen anything so beautiful in my entire life." Dube had been somewhat ready to do what Jae had said, but the vid put a steely resolve in his mind. Now he was determined to go forward.

The trio walked back to the kitchen door and faced the crowd. Dube addressed them. "Are you ready to go to the Registry and fight?"

The group all seemed to answer at the same time, some saying *yes*, others shouting *yes* or *amen*, others just whooping at seeing Dube and excited to get started. A smile spread across Dube's face as he saw that Cole and Abba would truly provide.

Dube spoke up. "Let's go then!" With Jae and Maj at his side, he walked toward the city as the crowd parted to let them through.

The same thing happened a few more times, where groups saw them coming and came out of hiding, or were standing on street corners and joined the group, or asked if this was Dube and then tagged along. By the time they came to the Registry, Jae estimated they were around three hundred strong. About the number of Gideon's army.[12]

I watched as my son fulfilled the Purpose I had tried to prepare him for. Well, technically, he wasn't my son anymore. He was always Abba's son, as all of the others were Abba's sons and daughters. He had only been on loan to me for the short time we were on Earth. For which I would be, literally, eternally grateful.

The Registry vizport was guarded by twice the number of Dube's company. And it was led by Tru. Not at all surprising to Dube that his first fight and his last were against the same person. He checked his left and right and saw that the remainder of the Boys were ready with swords drawn. He looked back at the group, and they all looked determined, equipped, and some, even thrilled. It was time.

With the words *"For Cole and Abba!"* ringing across the plaza, Dube led the charge straight at Seo's "army."

The broadsword felt comfortable in Dube's hands, a close companion he would be lost without. Tru was coming at him fast. Dube lifted the sword and swung, faintly aware of the sound of the blade slicing through the air, completely concentrated on the moment when the blade met its mark. As his enemy fell, Dube remembered his nightmare and all the times his life had ended in the dream on this field. It was only a moment. The battle sung around him, no time for contemplation. But he knew it would be all right. He knew his mother and father were safe. He and the Boys would free the port so everyone could get to the final battle, although it had already been won. He silently thanked Dr. Jay for all the prophecies drilled into his head that he now understood. This was the battle that had been fore-seen. This was Revelation. And lifting his sword for another swing, he whispered to himself, *"Dube! Breakfast!"*

Endnotes

1 I Corinthians 13:12
2 I Corinthians 6:12
3 Proverbs 21:9
4 Proverbs 18:24
5 Romans 12:19
6 Romans 8:29
7 Revelation 20:3
8 Isaiah 14:13
9 Luke 10:42
10 II Kings 2:11
11 I Corinthians 1:27
12 Judges 7:7

Endnotes

Acknowledgements

THANKS TO MY SISTERS, Rem and Rosi, and my good friends Lisa and Linda. We are not "the Boys" but "the Rust Girls". They edited and encouraged my efforts. Thanks to Kim for very early guidance, even if you don't remember giving it. Thanks to Pastor Jesse who pointed me to Mark Hitchcock's excellent tome on prophecy of the end times The End. Thanks to my husband who listened to plots, writing angst and issues endlessly - I love you. And a special thanks to Christopher John Chater, the real author in the extended family for helping me with resources and guidance.

All mistakes in writing and theology are mine. In the Spirit of this book I hope you will forgive them.

www.ingramcontent.com/pod-product-compliance
Lightning Source LLC
LaVergne TN
LVHW091158080426
835509LV00006B/740